HOW TO STOP PROCRASTINATING

A Cognitive Behavioral Therapy (CBT) Guide To Breaking The Procrastination Habit, Mastering Your Time, And Overcoming Your Negative Emotions

Antonio Matteo Bruscella

© Copyright 2019 by Antonio Matteo Bruscella

All rights reserved.

The reproduction, transmission, and duplication of any of the content found herein, including any specific or extended information will be done as an illegal act regardless of the end form the information ultimately takes. This includes copied versions of the work, both physical, digital, and audio unless the express consent of the Publisher is provided beforehand. Any additional rights reserved.

DEDICATION

To Paola e Michele for their amazing love and support.

A.M.B.

TABLE OF CONTENTS

Introduction	1
Chapter 1: Understanding Procrastination	6
The Science Behind Procrastination	6
Reasons Why People Procrastinate	9
Myths and Assumptions Regarding Procrastination	13
Benefits and Drawbacks of Procrastination	16
Drawbacks of Procrastination	17
Benefits of Procrastination	17
Consequences of Procrastination	18
Procrastinators Have Poorer Health Compared to Non-Procrastinators	18
Procrastinators Underachieve	19
Lower Life Satisfaction	19
Chapter 2: Understanding Cognitive Behavioral Therapy	21
How Does Cognitive Behavioral Therapy Work?	21
When Is Cognitive Behavioral Therapy Used?	24
CBT vs. Other Types of Therapies	25
Chapter 3: Changing Procrastination	27
The Vicious Cycle of Procrastination	27
What Causes Procrastination?	28
How to Overcome Procrastination	33
Chapter 4: Dismissing Procrastination Excuses	38

Common Procrastination Excuses	38
Testing Your Excuses	41
Defeating These Excuses	43
Worksheet #4.1 Sentence Completion Worksheet	44
Chapter 5: CBT Techniques to Stop Procrastination	47
Using CBT to Be Mindful of Your Thoughts	47
Unhelpful Thinking Styles	48
Identifying Your Own Unhelpful Thinking Patterns	50
Challenging Your Unhelpful Thinking Styles	51
Worksheet #5.1 Dysfunctional Thought Record	54
Worksheet #5.2 Cognitive Restructuring	56
Chapter 6: Challenges of Overcoming Procrastination	58
Your Inner-Critic	58
Breaking Out of Bad Habits	61
Unhelpful Thinking Styles	63
Learning About Your Inner-Critic	64
Question Your Inner-Critic	64
Worksheet #6.1 Training Your Inner-Critic (Four-Step Guide)	66
Chapter 7: The Power of Getting Started	79
How to Use CBT and Your Inner-Critic to Prevent Procrastination (7 Step Guide)	80
Step 1: Mindfulness	80
Step 2: Pay Attention to Your Thoughts	81
Step 3: Catch Your Own Unhelpful Thinking Patterns	82
Step 4: Challenge Your Unhelpful Thoughts With Evidence-Based Arguments	82
Step 5: Challenge Your Inner-Critic	83
Step 6: Negotiate With Your Inner-Critic	84
Step 7: Teach Your Inner-Critic to Be Supportive	84
Conclusion	86
Appendix	89
Recommended readings	105
About the author	108

INTRODUCTION

Procrastination is a term that is widely used all around the world. You have probably heard this most commonly in school or work. Procrastination is something that is so widely common that there are whole industries like the self-help that is worth over $9 billion dollars full of programs, books, and material to help people overcome it. If you are someone that is suffering from the effects of procrastination, you don't need to fret. Procrastination is a challenge that everyone has been faced with at some point in their lives. For as long as the human race has existed, people have struggled with avoiding, delaying, and procrastinating on the things and tasks that matter most to them.

When we are having our most productive moments, the moments where we have temporarily figured out how to overcome procrastination, we often find ourselves feeling accomplished and satisfied. Throughout this book, we will be learning about procrastination and everything that comes with it. You will get to learn what exactly procrastination is, the causes of it, common myths, and the many, many consequences of it. We will then learn about one of the most effective therapies in the psychology world today, Cognitive Behavioral Therapy (CBT). This is the most popular therapy on the market right now that is used to treat a variety of things like anxiety disorders, depression, self-esteem, and you guessed it, procrastination.

So let's start diving a little bit into procrastination. The human race has been procrastinating for many years. This problem is actually so well-known and timeliness that the ancient Greek philosophers like Aristotle and Socrates actually created a word to describe procrastination: Akrasia. Akrasia means the 'state of acting against your better judgment.' It's meaning is that of when a person is doing something, although they know that they ought to be doing something else. A loose translation of this is that akrasia is simply a lack of self-control. The modern definition of procrastination today is 'the act of delaying or postponing a task or set of tasks. Ultimately, whether you refer to procrastination as procrastination or akrasia, or maybe even something else, it all leads to the same meaning, which is the 'force' that is preventing you from doing the things that you had set yourself up to do.

So now that we have a brief understanding of the meaning of procrastination let's talk a little about Cognitive Behavioral Therapy. The term CBT has exponentially increased in popularity over the last ten years. People who have used CBT in the past know exactly what it is, but for the people who don't, you might be wondering, 'what is this?'. Cognitive-behavioral therapy is a type of speaking/talking therapy that is normally used to treat people with mental health or behavioral problems. The foundation of CBT is based on three cornerstone elements, which are cognition, emotion, and behavior. Cognition is responsible for how people think, emotion is based on how people feel, and behavior is based on how people act.

The theory of CBT is that the three components work hand in hand together, which ultimately determines a person's actions. A person's cognition (thoughts) affects their emotions, which then affects their behavior and actions. This means that when a person's thoughts are negative, unproductive, or unrealistic, it can cause a lot of distress in a person's life and will result in behavioral problems. When a person is suffering from any sort of psychological distress, they begin to perceive situations and life in a contorted manner, which then affects their actions.

To give you a little bit of a further understanding of CBT, let's talk briefly about the history of it. CBT is actually an umbrella term for numerous other kinds of therapies that share similar components. The earliest documented forms of CBT were developed by two psychologists named Albert Ellis and Aaron T. Beck back in the mid-90s. During this time, CBT was actually called Rational Emotive Behavior Therapy (REBT). REBT was developed to be a kind of cognitive therapy that focuses on fixing human emotional and behavioral problems. REBT's main goal was to change irrational beliefs that a person has into rational ones. This type of therapy was focused on encouraging a person to figure out what their irrational beliefs were and then help influence the individual to challenge those beliefs by testing them out in real life.

Knowing this information, you can see clearly why CBT is often used for overcoming procrastination. Since procrastination is when a person decides to do something that is not the task that they had set for themselves, it is likely due to some sort of unhealthy thinking style. By using CBT, you can begin identifying what those unhealthy thoughts and thinking styles are and begin influencing your own thoughts to help create emotions that will positively affect your behaviors.

In modern-day society, Cognitive Behavioral Therapy is most commonly used to treat mental disorders such as anxiety and depression. However, due to its many uses, professionals in the psychology space discovered that it could be used for many more things such as; increasing self-esteem, alcohol dependency, personality disorders, bulimia, and lastly, procrastination. Since CBT had such a long history and development, its modern-day form is a practical and time-saving form of psychotherapy. Rather than focusing on the history and childhood of the client, CBT focuses on their here-and-now problems that come up in their daily life. It is often used to help give an understanding to people regarding their sense of surroundings and events that happen to them and around them. The way CBT is structured is to be very problem-focused and time-saving. These many advantages are the main reasons as to why CBT is the most popular techniques used today to help people with the disorders that we mentioned above.

Throughout this book, we will be focusing on three main topics; procrastination, cognitive behavioral therapy, and your inner-critic. We will start off by learning about the science behind procrastination, why people procrastinate so often, myths and assumptions regarding procrastination, the benefits, and drawbacks of procrastination and the consequences of it. Once you get a good grasp of the details regarding procrastination, we will move on to learning more about CBT and how it actually works. We will learn a little bit regarding when CBT is used and how it compares to some of the other therapies that can be used to treat behavioral problems. Towards the center of this book, we will begin learning more about procrastination. We will be exploring topics such as; the vicious cycle of procrastination and how to break out it, the causes of procrastination, and you will be given tips and simple instructions on how to overcome procrastination without CBT. We will also learn about the common excuses that people make for themselves when they procrastinate, and we will learn about how we can begin identifying those excuses and how to overcome them. You will also be provided with a few worksheets throughout these chapters to help you practice overcoming common procrastination obstacles. Towards the end of the book, you will be taught some practical techniques using CBT to help prevent procrastination. You will learn about all the unhelpful thinking patterns that people often have unconsciously, how to identify what are yours, and learning to interrupt them. You will also be provided with some worksheets in these chapters to get some practice in. Once you get a good handle on the CBT techniques, we will introduce a topic regarding your inner-critic. We will learn what an inner-critic is, how to identify the things it is saying to you, beginning to question your inner-critic, and then training the inner-critic to be supportive rather than critical. In our last chapter, we will be learning about how we can use CBT on a daily basis to control and prevent procrastination altogether. You will then be provided by a step by step guide of using a combination of CBT and inner-critic techniques to battle procrastination. You will also be provided with more worksheets to help with practice.

The purpose of this book is to arm you with all the correct tools so you can help yourself when it comes to procrastination. By understanding the psychology and science behind procrastination and CBT, you are able to create the necessary buy-in for yourself to continue practicing its methodologies. Keep in mind that this book is designed to educate you regarding the topics of procrastination and CBT. However, this book is not designed as a substitute for proper diagnosis, treatment, or advice by a health professional. If you believe that your symptoms are severe or if you have been diagnosed by a doctor before regarding your symptoms, then I urge you to have an assessment conducted by a health professional.

CHAPTER 1: UNDERSTANDING PROCRASTINATION

The purpose of this chapter is to give you a detailed look into what exactly procrastination is, the psychology behind it, reasons why people procrastinate, bust some common myths, and learn about some of the long-term consequences of procrastination. Just to reiterate, we just learned the modern definition of procrastination, which is 'the act of delaying or postponing a task or set of tasks. Let's learn a little about why people procrastinate. What exactly is going on in the human brain that causes people to avoid doing the things that they KNOW they should be doing?

The Science Behind Procrastination

Through an abundance of psychology research, psychologists have discovered a phenomenon called "time inconsistency," which helps explain why procrastination affects humans so largely by pulling us away from needed tasks despite our good intentions. The term time inconsistency refers to the habit of the human mind to value immediate gratification or rewards more highly compared to long-term and future rewards. The best way to further understand this is to imagine that you have two alter egos. The first is your present self, and the second is your future self. When a person sets goals for themselves, such as getting fit by working out more or learning a new language, they are actually making plans for their future self. They are envisioning what they want their life to be like in the future. Evidence has shown researchers that when a person thinks about their future self, it is not difficult for their brain to see the value of doing actions that will lead to long-term benefits. The future self is the one that values long-term rewards.

On the contrary, while the future self can only set goals, the present self is the one that is responsible for taking action. There will come a time where this individual will need to make a decision, but they aren't making a choice for the future self at this point. In the present moment, their brain is focused entirely on the present self. Research shows that the present self prefers immediate rewards over long-term ones. This means that the present self and future self don't often get along. While the future wants to be healthy and have a six-pack, the present self wants some chili cheese fries. Everyone knows that eating unhealthily will prevent health problems in the future when you're at an old age, but those things are so far away, so why worry about them now, right? This is the thought process that many people have when they are faced with a choice of immediate gratification or achieving long-term goals.

Very similarly, most young people know that saving money for their retirement during their 20s and 30s is extremely valuable, but the benefit of this is many decades away. It is much easier for a person's present-self to see value in buying themselves a new iPhone rather than putting away $1000 for their 75-year-old self! This concept of "time inconsistency" may be the reason why people often go to bed feeling motivated and inspired to reach their goals and change their life but they find themselves completely falling back into bad habits when they wake up. This is due to the fact that the human brain values long-term benefits when they are thinking about the future, but it prefers immediate gratification when it comes to the present moment. Let's dive into a little bit more of the science behind this.

For the sake of example here, let's pretend for a little while that you are a giraffe living in the plains of the African savanna. Your neck is 6 feet long, and occasionally you will see a group of human tourists driving in a car with a safari tour taking pictures of you. However, it's not just your long neck that separates you from the humans. It could be that the biggest difference between you and your other giraffe friends and the humans taking pictures is that almost every single decision that you make brings an immediate benefit to your life. For example, when you see a storm coming, you will find shelter under a tree, or if you are hungry, you walk over to the nearest tree and begin to eat, or when you spot a predator hunting you, you begin to run away.

Every day, most of the choices that you make as a giraffe, such as where to sleep when to avoid a predator or what to eat, make a direct and immediate impact on your life. You are entirely focused on the present, and the furthest you would think about is the near future. You are living in an 'Immediate-Return Environment'; this is what scientists call this environment due to the fact that your actions deliver very immediate and clear outcomes.

Now let's change things up and pretend that you are one of the human tourists that are traveling in Africa on the safari. Different from giraffes, humans live in a 'Delayed Return Environment.' Most of the choices made in this type of environment will not benefit you right away. For example, if you save your money now, you'll have enough for retirement in forty years, or if you work hard at your job today, you will get paid in two weeks. Rewards are designed to be delayed until some point in the future in many aspects of modern-day society.

While the giraffe is worried about problems that are immediate, such as avoiding predators, seeking shelters, and finding food, humans worry the most about the problems of the future. For instance, while the humans are on the safari, they may be thinking, "This trip and safari has been tremendous fun! It would be so awesome if I could work as a safari tour guide and be able to see the giraffes every day. Speaking of work, is it time for me to change my career? Am I really working the kind of job that I enjoy? Should I start looking for new jobs?" Unfortunately for us, humans that are living in a Delayed Return Environment tend to lead to a lot of anxiety and stress. This is because the human brain wasn't designed to solve problems of a Delayed Return Environment. In fact, this is why there has been a rise in depression and anxiety over the last decade. Where people of the past focused more on their immediate problems like harvesting their crops for food or boiling water, so it's safe to drink, people nowadays focus on problems that are in the future since most of our basic needs are already taken care of.

Reasons Why People Procrastinate

Let's learn a little about why people procrastinate. Most people are more than capable of achieving great things in their life, but many fail to do so. Procrastination is probably one of the biggest obstacles that hinder a person from being able to achieve greater things. Everyone has procrastinated before, and anyone is capable of it. Many times, people don't even know that they are procrastinating. However, there are also those moments where people know that they are procrastinating but fail to do anything to stop the process. So why do people procrastinate anyways, although they are self-aware? There are numerous reasons why people begin procrastinating; let's take a look at the most common ones:

Skill Deficiency

In order for a person to achieve their goals, it requires them to learn and to have personal growth. People will have to develop new skills and knowledge related to their set goals. This is a huge part of their journey. However, people often fail to see this fact. They see their lack of skill or knowledge as an obstacle that is permanent and cannot be overcome. This mindset causes people to give up on their goals before they have even done anything to start it. Rather than giving up, people need to be able to assess the skills and knowledge that are required to achieve their goal and then compare it to their own skills and knowledge that they possess.

The difference between the two is nothing more than just an opportunity to learn and train. Instead of just giving up, people need to create a plan that will help them develop and learn the skills needed in order to bridge that gap. So is it procrastination if you are pushing the date of your goal achievement back? Absolutely not. This is just effective planning. By understanding that you require more time to reach your goal means that you are identifying the right steps you need to take to reach your goal.

Lack of interest

Everyone has their own special set of interests. Just because your friend is passionate about a particular topic or job, it does not mean that everyone else is interested in the same thing. People have the tendency to put off doing jobs that they do not find interesting because it is more difficult to find motivation. There are multiple ways that people can deal with jobs that they have no interest in depending on if you are the person that is actually doing the job or if they are the person that is simply assigning the task. Let's take a look at the perspective of a person that is physically doing the job; they could try the following things:

- Check to see if this task actually has to be done
- Ask yourself if there is someone else who is much better suited to completing this task. If possible, you may be able to swap it or delegate it (e.g., if someone else likes that job better, you can trade with them for theirs that you might like better)
- If your tolerance for frustration is low, try to break down this job into smaller pieces and complete them one at a time
- If your tolerance for frustration is higher, you can schedule a block of time where you take away all distractions and just do this task until it is done

From the perspective of the person who is assigning the job/task, you will likely find more success if you assign this specific task to someone who you know will be passionate about it. By choosing someone who has an interest in that task, the job will be completed in a much faster fashion and at a higher standard as well.

Lack of motivation

People often have the wrong mindset where they think that they need to feel fully motivated before they start working on a task/job. This mindset is unrealistic. People's motivation often does not arrive until they have started that task and is beginning to see progress. When people see progress, they start to see the fruits to their labor, and they become even more motivated to keep working until they have completed their task. You might be wondering what about the motivation that is needed in order to start working altogether? The answer to this is that a person needs to have a good understanding of the 'why' and the vision of that particular job. Before you even begin working on it, you should know what the benefits are going to be. You would be surprised at how many people waste a lot of time doing work that actually does not need to be completed. Moreover, people should be using prioritization in order to get the most urgent and important work out of the way first. By understanding the benefits of completing a task or job, you will fully be able to estimate its importance. In terms of smaller tasks/jobs, simply understanding what the benefits are of completing that task should be enough for motivation. For larger tasks and jobs, it is important that you have a way to measure your progress so you can further gain motivation and confidence from your work.

Fear of failure

There are a lot of people who have the belief that failure is devastating. They often see failure as a final result that is set in stone and cannot be rectified or changed. Failure to them is a permanent stain on their reputation, which means that every time that they fail, their ego takes a huge hit. This lack of confidence causes them to avoid taking action on tasks where they are not 100% absolutely confident in its success. Keep in mind that in the era that we live in today, many tasks that people face will be new to them, and it is entirely impossible to be able to be 100% confident in every single chance of success. Due to this, procrastination is something that happens frequently and in an endless spiral.

On the contrary, there are the people out there who see failure as a stepping stone towards success and a learning opportunity. They have the understanding and belief that mistakes are unavoidable, and they will be made. Their attitude consists mostly of realistic optimism, which enables them to believe that they will be able to successfully achieve their goal/task even if it's something that requires more than one try. As you might be able to tell, these types of people have a much lower tendency to procrastinate. Instead, they often approach new challenges with excitement and preparedness to deal with obstacles.

Since learning and growth are important parts of a successful life, it is unrealistic to believe that you can succeed without experiencing any obstacles or failures in your journey. If you are constantly worrying and are scared at the idea of failure, try to identify extra steps or measures that you can take in order to lower the chances of failure and increase the chances of success. Factor in time that you can take to review and assess your own actions and try to learn something from every experience. You will soon start to change your mindset into one where you see every challenge as an opportunity for learning and growth.

Fear of success

Many professionals of the self-help industry have talked or theorized about the fact that people's biggest fear wasn't necessarily a failure, but our biggest fear is actually the fear of success. Many people view success as stress and pressure. When they think about achieving greater and more things, they often think about the negative aspects that come with it. For example, they believe that when a person achieves more, people will begin to demand and expect more from you. They often doubt their ability to deal with the increased expectations, so they decide to procrastinate to sabotage their own chances of success.

The reality here is that there is no reason that a person should fear success. As a person begins to succeed by overcoming the challenges of all difficulties, they begin to become more knowledgeable and have developed new skills. Their resilience will begin to increase. If a person is able to learn the necessary skills of personal organization, it really doesn't matter what type of task or work that they are doing, they will be able to find a way through. Long story short, every task is simply just a task that needs to be completed. When you are able to break down every large task into a number of smaller tasks, there should be nothing that would be able to overwhelm you.

Resistance

You might have experienced this phenomenon before, where there are times that it would be easier for you to just complete a task than procrastinate but yet you still chose to procrastinate! The main reason for this is rebellion. There is a class of procrastinators called the 'rebellious procrastinators.' They are very common. These people deliberately delay tasks, defy standards, falter expectations, and impedes protocol. This type of procrastination can be done by anyone, especially if they feel like they have been mistreated.

The reasons that cause people to procrastinate are different for every individual. The exact reason why for each individual, may not be obvious, but the obvious reasons may be caused by something that is underlying. On the contrary, the reasons that we had just discussed are seen as the most common ones. Trying to avoid this type of behavior is not an easy task as it often involves a person to identify their bad habits and actively try to break them down and create new ones. Whether you are the procrastinator or you are suffering at the hands of one, the important part here is to take action immediately. You have to take action in order to correct your situation. Keep in mind that procrastination is a serious issue that, if left unresolved for a long time, can cause some serious and long-lasting problems in your life.

Myths and Assumptions Regarding Procrastination

Let's begin to learn about some of the most common myths and assumptions regarding procrastination. By learning about what these are, we can get those false ideas out of our minds and focus on facts. There are numerous myths and excuses that people tell themselves in order to avoid work that needs to be done. In fact, so many excuses that we will have a whole chapter dedicated to talking about this later on in the book. Below are four of the most common myths regarding procrastination.

1. "I work better under pressure."

Think about this for a second that you have an important work report that is due to your boss in two weeks. Instead of starting the report, you find yourself doing other unnecessary things like reorganizing your stamp collection or cleaning your bathtub. In order to reduce the disagreement between what you should be doing and what you are actually doing, you start to rationalize your behavior. You begin telling yourself that you are just the type of person who works better 'under pressure' so the best thing that you can do for yourself is to delay the start of your report.

The hard reality here is that procrastination is actually harmful to a person's performance. Last-minute scrambling around to get tasks and jobs done or cramming the night before a final exam is not efficient or enjoyable. When people plan and pace their projects, it typically gets them better results, and it is a whole lot less stressful than pulling all-nighters to get things done. If you are someone who is absolutely convinced that they can't start working on a task unless you are feeling the pressure of a close deadline, then you can try to fix this habit by creating artificial pressure of yourself. There are a few ways that you can approach this technique. For instance, you can set a 30-minute timer and tell yourself that you only have 30 minutes to write the opening paragraph of your report. You can convince yourself that the report that you have to write is timed and that at the end of the 30-minute timer, you have to stop writing. You could also try asking a friend to be your 'accountability buddy' who is someone that you have to 'hand in' your work to.

2. "I need to be inspired or feeling motivated before I can begin working."

People often put off doing certain tasks until they're 'in the mood' or 'feeling inspired.' By telling yourself that you are waiting for a certain emotion to come is really just procrastination in disguise. Rather than waiting for a certain emotion to come before getting started on your task/work, you need to tell yourself that this work needs to be done regardless of how much or little inspiration you feel. By doing this, you will find that inspiration is a product of discipline. When you begin to start working on the task that you've set, you will start feeling fulfilled, which then leads to actual inspiration. Simply just stop wasting time waiting for the feeling of inspiration to hit you. Just like Picasso once said, "Inspiration exists, but it has to find you working."

3. "I need to have at least 3 – 4 hours of uninterrupted time to work on this."

People often believe in the myth that they need a certain huge chunk of uninterrupted time to be able to accomplish whatever they are looking to accomplish. However, if a person doesn't have that a long chunk of time to work on their task, such as that report that's due in two weeks, then they are making a mistake by delaying their task until they find themselves with a few hours of uninterrupted time. Rather than doing this, you should try to apply a technique called the "Swiss Cheese Approach." Since Swiss cheese is a type of cheese that is famous for its numerous holes, the Swiss cheese approach means that is possible for a person to get something that starts in just 5 minutes or less. Once a person has started, they have actually opened up their own opportunity to keep it going.

The Swiss Cheese Approach is made of the following elements:
- Try working in small 'holes' of time. Try getting some work done in just 15, 20, or 30 minutes.
- Work away at large tasks by poking small 'holes' consistently.

This approach is efficient because of these reasons:
- Once you actually start working on a task, it no longer feels as overwhelming or difficult as it did before you actually started.
- By poking small 'holes' in a task that you're doing, you'll be making small but constant progress.
- This approach will help you build a sense of 'forward momentum'; once you start, you are motivated to keep doing more.
- Each time that you complete a small amount of the task that needs to be done, it will give you a sense of accomplishment.
- You are making good use of small portions of time rather than wasting it completely.

The next time you find yourself with only 15 – 20 minutes of time to work on your task/project, rather than telling yourself that you don't have enough time or waiting until you have a longer time block, ask yourself these questions below:
- "Is there a small 'hole' in this project that I can start with?"
- "How can I use this time to poke a small 'hole' in my task?"
- "What can I get done in 10 – 15 minutes?"

By continuing to poke 'holes' into your tasks and projects whenever you find yourself with some time to spare, you will be surprised to find that you have accomplished a lot of your task.

4. "I'll be able to do this job better tomorrow."

Everyone has the tendency to believe that things will be different in the future, even if the 'future' means tomorrow. The mindset is often "In the future; I'll have more time and be better organized. In the future, I'll have more energy and be more well-rested, so I can get things done." Due to this, people often pass over their present-day responsibilities over to their future selves, not knowing that they probably won't be that much different from now. Here are a few items that you need to consider; firstly, unless you actively start taking action needed to be more effective and productive right now, you'll be in the exact same situation tomorrow. Second, unless you are doing the necessary actions to increase your discipline in the present moment, you will be just as undisciplined tomorrow. Lastly, unless you are taking steps to become more organized right now, you will be at the same level of disorganization tomorrow. All of this can be summarized in just one sentence; don't put off things for tomorrow that you can do today.

Almost all of us have at least truly believed in one of those four myths as a way to be excused from completing tasks/work that didn't make us feel comfortable. It could be because we have a fear of doing a bad job, or that task seemed too complex, or we were feeling overwhelmed, or simply just because there was something else 'better' to do.

Benefits and Drawbacks of Procrastination

You're probably wondering by the title of this chapter, benefits, and drawbacks of procrastination? Sure, there are a ton of drawbacks of procrastination, but what benefits are there? Well, I can tell you right now, not many. However, I'd be lying if I told you there were none, but they are very few, and they are not common. Let's start with the drawbacks of procrastination first.

Drawbacks of Procrastination

1. Stress is one of the biggest drawbacks of procrastination. When a person realizes that there is a specific task or work that they need to do, the tendency is to think about that task until it is completed. Other people may forget about it and may remember at the last minute that they still need to complete this task. No matter the personality of the person, everyone will feel the stress of procrastination at some point in their lives.
2. Not being able to do the task to your full ability is another drawback. Since the task or job that you needed to do was done at the very last minute, it may be sloppily completed and is not reflective of your true potential. Give yourself more time so that you can use it better and showcase your best efforts.
3. A common drawback is an anxiety. Similar to stress, some people constantly worry about a task or project, and they make all these excuses to not do it until the very last minute. Even though they completed the project in the end, they are likely very mentally exhausted. They spent so much time and energy thinking about this task rather than just doing it. They probably spent more time thinking about it than actually doing it!
4. Disorganization is another huge drawback of procrastination. When someone is constantly procrastinating all the tasks they need to do, they end up with a huge laundry list of items and don't have the required time to complete everything.

Benefits of Procrastination

Although there are very few benefits to procrastination, there are just a couple that is worth talking about.

1. Being under pressure can be a good thing for certain types of people when it comes to completing tasks. For this small and might I mention, very rare, group of people, waiting until the last minute to finish something helps motivate them to do it well. For some people, working pressure can actually help them succeed, but this does NOT apply to everyone. I know we just talked about how "I work better under pressure" is a myth, and

I still believe it is. However, I can't deny that there is a small group of people out there that are capable of delivering good quality work when they are under pressure.
2. Another benefit is that sometimes, it is not necessary to do certain tasks or work until the day before the deadline. Worrying about it could actually be more of a hassle because you know for a fact that this work will get done. Certain types of people don't need to complete things early in order to get the stress off their shoulders. In fact, they might not have been stressed in the first place at all if they were confident that this task would get done before the deadline.

Consequences of Procrastination

If the purpose of this book is to help you overcome procrastination long-term, then it is very important for us to talk about what the consequences of procrastination are. Everyone knows that procrastination is never a good thing, but not many people know the specifics to the actual consequences of it. By understanding some of the very real consequences that procrastinating can cause, it will help motivate you to actively work to overcome it.

Procrastinators Have Poorer Health Compared to Non-Procrastinators

This may come as a surprise to some, but non-procrastinators are healthier than procrastinators. There is a multitude of reasons. To start off, procrastinators tend to put off important tasks related to health such as; regular checkups, treatments, colonoscopies, etc. You see the point. Often, procrastinators are anxious regarding their health, and therefore, they put off seeing the doctor for a check-up to avoid the risk of hearing that they have a disease that is too advanced to be cured.

Besides the fact that procrastinators are more likely to put off important health appointments, the act of procrastination itself puts a lot of unnecessary burden on our immune system and bodies. This is caused by an increased amount of stress and other negative emotions such as guilt, anxiety, shame, and self-criticism. In addition, lifelong procrastinators tend to delay healthy behaviors, such as getting enough sleep, exercising, and eating healthy. Due to the constant need to pull all-nighters and eating extraordinary amounts of junk food may not be a huge deal in the short term, but over a long period of time, it will result in serious health conditions like heart disease and diabetes. This doesn't even include issues such as productivity, longevity, vitality, loss in energy, and so forth! Since lack of self-control is one of the reasons that procrastination happens to some people, procrastinators have a higher chance of engaging in activities that are known to provide instant gratification but may cause physical harm if done too often Examples of this would be excessive alcohol use, smoking, drug abuse…etc.

Procrastinators Underachieve

This one is probably quite obvious to most. It is not surprising that procrastinators tend to do worse compared to their non-procrastinating peers in school, work, or anywhere where performance is measured. If you are someone who is often procrastinating, you probably are self-aware to know that you are operating and working below your potential. Often, non-procrastinators are planning ahead and trying to make the most use of their time while procrastinators are more likely to engage in instant gratification like browsing the web on their phone, playing video games, watching TV or anything that causes a distraction from whatever they are supposed to be doing.

Lower Life Satisfaction

At this point, you can probably guess what I'm about to say next. Procrastinators are less happy than those who don't procrastinate. There are numerous reasons for this. To start off, procrastinators are likely to be less successful compared to non-procrastinators in many areas of life, including career, health, and relationships. This is due to the fact that they tend to avoid doing the things that need to be done in order to advance themselves in those areas of life. Non-procrastinators spend less time doing activities that benefit them in the short term, but they focus more on doing the activities that will benefit them in the long term.

In addition, people who procrastinate are often very self-critical.

Just like we talked about earlier in this book, a lot of people may be procrastinating because they are afraid that they can't execute a certain task or job perfectly. Due to this avoidance, they can't get themselves to do the things that they know will benefit them and end up beating themselves up because of it. During the moments of fear regarding those mental beatings, they often sabotage themselves, which results in them having even less productivity. It's not easy to be happy when a person is living in a state of constant self-criticism and disappointment.

Next, there is the constant guilt that procrastinators feel. Often people already feel guilty regardless of what they do, but if some needless procrastination is added into the mix, then the guilt can easily become overwhelming. When someone is doing something that is not what they know they're supposed to be doing, they are often very aware of the guilt that they are feeling during those times. It's like a cloud that is constantly looming over their heads, reminding them of what a bad person they are because of how much procrastination they are exhibiting. Since they feel like they are not productive, they often may feel that they don't deserve any time off. This creates an endless cycle of guilt, procrastination, and self-loathing. It's tough to feel happy when those are the constant emotions that a person is feeling.

CHAPTER 2: UNDERSTANDING COGNITIVE BEHAVIORAL THERAPY

At this point in the book, you should have a solid foundation of knowledge regarding what procrastination is and some of its negative consequences. We talked about Cognitive Behavioral Therapy very briefly at the beginning of this book, but this chapter will be focused entirely on what exactly CBT is and how it works. Just to reiterate, the cornerstones of CBT are made up of three elements; cognition (thought), emotion, and behavior. These three components all interact with one another, which leads to the theory that a person's thoughts determine their emotions, which then determines their behavior.

How Does Cognitive Behavioral Therapy Work?

CBT functions by emphasizing the relationship between a person's thoughts, feelings, and behaviors. When a person begins to change one of these components, you begin to start initiating change to the others. The goal of CBT is to help a person identify any unhelpful thoughts or thinking patterns that may be lowering their quality of life. In our case, we will be utilizing CBT in order to fix the unhealthy thinking styles that lead to procrastination. Here are a few basic principles regarding how CBT works:

1. CBT will help provide a new perspective of understanding of your problems.

When someone has been living with a certain problem, like procrastination, for a long period of time, they usually have developed their own unique ways of understanding it, perceiving it, and dealing with it. Usually, these ways that they have adopted are not healthy, and usually, it just makes the problem worse or simply maintains it. CBT is very effective in helping people look at their problems from a different perspective and will aid you in learning other ways of understanding your problem and finding a new solution to deal with it.

2. CBT will help you generate new skills to work out your problem.

Most people probably know that understanding a problem is one matter, but dealing with it is a whole other beast. To begin initiating change for your problem, you will need to develop a new set of skills that will aid you in changing your thoughts, behaviors, and emotions that are affecting your productivity. For instance, CBT will help you come up with new ideas related to your problem, and you can begin to test these ideas in your day to day life. Therefore, a person will now be more capable of making up their own mind regarding the root issue that is causing these negative symptoms and/or behavior.

3. CBT relies on teamwork and collaboration between the therapist (or program).

CBT is a type of therapy that requires you to be actively involved in the entire process. The client's thoughts and ideas are very valuable right from the start of therapy. The only expert is you when it comes to your own thoughts and problems. The therapist (or the CBT program you are following) is the expert when it comes to acknowledging emotional issues. With the client and therapist/program working as one unit, the client will be able to identify what their problems are and have the therapist/program help them address it. Historically, the more that this therapy advances, the more the client takes the lead when it comes to finding techniques to deal with symptoms and behaviors.

4. The goal of CBT is to help the client become their own therapist.

Therapy is expensive, and if your goal is to overcome procrastination, getting a therapist may not be worth it. One of the main goals of CBT is to make sure that the client does not become overly dependent on their therapist because it isn't feasible to go to therapy forever. When therapy comes to an end, and this person has not become their own therapist, they are likely at high risk for a relapse. However, if you are able to be your own therapist, you will place yourself in a good spot in order to overcome the obstacles that life will throw at you. In our case, it is unrealistic for you to go running to your support system whenever you procrastinate. Instead, CBT will give you the tools that you need in order to moderate your actions to help you stay on track. By playing an active role during the CBT process, you will be able to gain the confidence needed in order to overcome any procrastination that you will be faced with.

5. CBT is direction based and structured.

The fundamental strategy of CBT is 'guided recovery.' By setting up some experiments with your therapist or CBT program, you will be able to test out new ideas to see if they are working with your own reality. In other words, your program or therapist is your guide as you are making discoveries about yourself through the use of CBT. Your program or therapist is not here to tell you whether you are right or wrong, but instead, they help you develop ideas and experiments so you can test them out for yourself.

6. CBT is based on the present, "here and now."

Unlike different therapies, one of the main principles of CBT is that it distinguished the difference between what caused a certain problem and what is presently maintain that problem. In most cases, the reasons that a problem is being maintained is different than the reasons that had originally caused it. For instance, if a person falls off while horseback riding, they may become afraid of horses. Their fear will become maintained if all they do is avoid horses and refuse to ride one ever again. In this example, the fear itself was caused by the fall and not the horse itself. By avoiding the fear, the person is continuing to maintain it and allowing it to be a part of their life. CBT focuses on the factors that maintain a certain problem because these are the factors that are most susceptible to change. Using a procrastination-based example, if you once got a bad mark on a paper you wrote in university, you may avoid writing one in the future because you think you're bad at it. However, you may not be considering some of the external factors that could be affecting your grade, such as the course itself, the professor, the environment that you wrote it in, the topic, etc. By avoiding writing your paper, you are maintaining the problem. You aren't actually afraid of writing the paper itself; you are actually just afraid of getting a bad grade. Do you see the difference?

7. Worksheet exercises are significant elements of CBT Therapy.

Just simply reading about CBT, following a program, or going to one session of therapy per week is not enough to change a person's ingrained patterns of thinking and habits of behaving. The client is always encouraged to apply the new skills into their daily lives during the course of CBT. Although most people find the concept of CBT to be very intriguing, it does not change their reality if they don't actually apply the skills that they have learned.

When Is Cognitive Behavioral Therapy Used?

Let's learn a little about when CBT is actually used. The main answer here is that CBT is used when a person decides to pursue help either through therapy or a self-help program in order to help with the problems they are facing. In our case, we will be using CBT in order to overcome procrastination, but a lot of the time, people are looking to overcome more serious problems such as anxiety, depression, or disorders such as OCD and PTSD.

The most common uses of CBT are for depression and generalized anxiety disorder. CBT can also be very effective for these following disorders:
- Eating Disorders
- Chronic Low Back Pain

- Body Dysmorphic Disorder
- Personality Disorder
- Schizophrenia
- Psychosis
- Substance Abuse Disorders

Since the main theory of CBT is to focus on the relationship between a person's thoughts, emotions, and behaviors, people who are suffering from a mental disorder may find CBT very useful. Most therapists in our present time choose CBT as the first technique to deal with any problems that their client may be facing, as CBT covers such a broad range of disorders. The client will be able to learn CBT and continue to use it for themselves without the help of the therapist.

On a simpler note, CBT can also be used for general therapy. This is suitable for our case where we are using CBT to break out of bad habits to overcome procrastination. Some people may use it to simply be more in touch with their own thoughts and feelings. Even if a person is not actually suffering from any sort of disorder, CBT can still be a very helpful tool for someone that is looking to organize their thoughts.

CBT vs. Other Types of Therapies

Cognitive Behavioral Therapy and other kinds of behavioral therapies have a lot of similarities, but also a lot of significant differences. The kind of behavioral therapy that we typically see on TV and in movies may seem to involve the client talking a lot about their childhood or dream interpretations. This type of method is actually very outdated compared to the modern-day CBT. It is so outdated in fact that almost no therapists in the modern-day use this type of therapy anymore. CBT is unique on its own because of how it focuses entirely on the relationship between the person's thoughts, emotions, and behaviors.

The main theory behind CBT being that thoughts control feelings, and a person's emotional response to a situation comes from how they interpreted the situation. Here is an example that will help you understand a little bit further. Imagine feeling a physical sensation of an irregularly fast heartbeat, and you are struggling to breathe. If this occurred while you were sitting on your couch at home relaxing, you would likely assume that these feelings are due to a medical condition such as a heart problem. This will likely cause you to worry and have anxiety. On the contrary, if these symptoms occurred while you were running outside, you would not likely attribute those symptoms to a medical condition, and therefore, you will not feel the emotions of anxiety and worry. This example outlines how different interpretations of the exact same physical sensations can lead to an entirely different set of emotions.

CBT is a therapy that suggests that most people's emotions are completely caused by what they are thinking about. In other words, our emotions are based entirely on our perceptions and interpretations of our situation or environment. Sometimes the thoughts and ideas we have become biased or distorted. For instance, if you got an ambiguous text message, you may take it as a personal rejection when the text message doesn't actually have any evidence to support that thought. You may begin to set some unrealistic expectations for yourself in hopes of being accepted by others. These types of thoughts play a huge role in people's mindset by creating distorted, biased, and illogical thinking processes which largely effects our emotions. In CBT, individuals have the opportunity to distinguish the differences between their actual thoughts and feelings. Meanwhile, other types of behavioral therapies tend to focus more on a person's history rather than focusing on the relationship between thoughts and behavior.

Other types of behavioral therapies are very different from CBT because most of these therapies focus on how a person's certain thoughts and behaviors are accidentally presented with a 'reward' within their environment. By receiving a reward, it contributes to the increase of those thoughts and behaviors.

CHAPTER 3: CHANGING PROCRASTINATION

At this point in the book, we have a good idea of what procrastination is and how CBT can help with overcoming it. In this chapter, we will be learning about the vicious cycle of procrastination, how it's caused, and how we can break out of it. This chapter does not necessarily utilize the structured format of CBT, but once we learn more about CBT, you can include some of those techniques as well. You will be given a set of practical instructions for you to start overcoming procrastination in this chapter that does not require CBT. This can be used in the meantime while you are still learning the ropes for how CBT is used.

The Vicious Cycle of Procrastination

Procrastination arises from some of our own unhelpful rules and assumptions that we have of ourselves and the rest of the world. When these rules and assumptions are activated, they lead people to detect some sort of discomfort about doing a task or job that they've set up for themselves in the past. If the person is unable to tolerate this discomfort, they will likely utilize procrastination as a method of avoiding this discomfort. They often can come up with pretty convincing justifications or excuses for their procrastination, but they will be more likely to go down the route of procrastinating. Due to

...is, they will end up engaging in procrastination activities such as instant gratification things that create a pleasurable distraction that substitutes the task that they are supposed to be doing. In return, there are consequences that come up due to this procrastination, which will make the person more likely to go down the route of procrastination again the next time they are faced with a similar task or job. This cycle happens because people got a 'reward' or pay-off for their procrastination, and they have made that task even more aversive by avoiding it in the first place.

To help give you a visualization of this cycle, here is a little chart that will help explain it further.

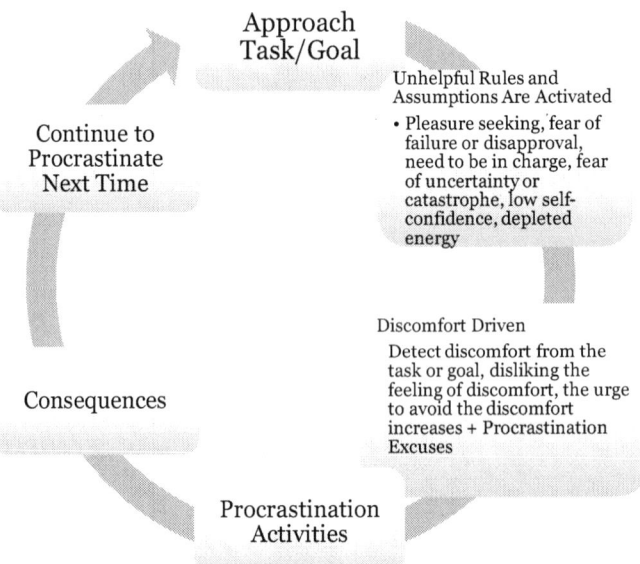

What Causes Procrastination?

We learned that the umbrella cause for procrastination is a person's feeling of 'discomfort' regarding a particular task or job. However, do we know what those discomforts maybe? One of the biggest challenges when it comes to overcoming procrastination is the fact that everyone has a different reason for doing it. Finding out what causes YOU specifically to procrastinate is the first step to getting to the bottom of the problem. Moreover, a person doesn't only have one cause that makes them procrastinate. In fact, one person can have a multitude of reasons for procrastinating different types of tasks. In this chapter, we will be studying the most common reasons and causes of procrastination and how to break out of it. At the end of this chapter, you will be provided with an 11-step guide to help you begin overcoming procrastination. Please note that this guide does not include technical CBT methods; we will learn a more technical guide later on in this book.

Cause #1: Perfectionism

One of the most common causes of procrastination is a person's need for perfectionism. The fear of making mistakes is a very common feeling that many people have that causes them to procrastinate on tasks that they know they need to do. A very famous psychologist wrote a book regarding procrastination and determined that people either have a fixed mindset or a growth mindset. People that have a fixed mindset believe that their abilities cannot be changed and that they are set in stone. They can only focus their current existing skills, talents, and intelligence and believe that those things cannot be further developed. Those that have a fixed mindset believe that they are born with what they have and that they don't have a way to improve their abilities. They also believe that effort is not required for success if a person has talent. They believe that talent is something that comes naturally. A fixed mindset is a dangerous thing because it hinders a person's ability to change, learn, grow, and to make positive changes.

Consequently, the growth mindset is one that allows a person to believe that skills, abilities, and intelligence are things that can be developed if you put in the hard work. They have the belief that a person's skills and talents are just their starting point. They believe that they are born with certain strengths, but there is no limit to what other strengths or goals they can accomplish if they put in the effort. The psychologists who studied this theory believe that people who procrastinate due to suffering from perfectionism often have a fixed mindset. What this means is that these people avoid doing the tasks that they need to do because they are afraid of the risk of making a mistake and accomplishing anything that's less than perfect. They want all of their work to be perfect because they believe that if a task is not

100% in line with their current skills/talents, then they will inevitably fail. Therefore, they put this task aside for another time where they feel more ready or capable.

Although perfectionism is often seen as a positive trait, it is actually something that is very detrimental. It is a trait that is built of anti-productive habits and attitudes that hinder a person's profession. Perfectionism is often misunderstood as someone having high standards, but the reality is that perfectionism holds unrealistic standards.

Cause #2: Fear of the Unknown

Often times, if a person is anxious, they are likely to be afraid of the unknown. People that have a fear of taking action are often scared of revealing the truth about something that they don't want to hear. Some people hold on to this old phrase, 'what you don't know can't hurt you.' However, this phrase is hugely untrue, and in almost every single case, if a person ignores something for a long time while hoping it will go away, that one thing will only definitely get worse. There was a study that was conducted by researchers at the University of Michigan that focused on studying the effects of misinformation lingering on a person's mind. The study found that misinformation is retained in a person's memory and continues to influence the way a person thinks even if they know that those thoughts are incorrect. The person was found also to be more likely to use the misinformation, especially if it's one that aligns with their current existing beliefs. This will then lead to spreading inaccurate information to others.

The researchers from this study found that a person's personal views and beliefs are a huge obstacle for helping this person change their mind about their believed misinformation. They found that attempting to show this person with the unwanted truth that is against what they believed previously can easily backfire and amplify their misinformed ideas even more. This is very dangerous when it comes to a person's health issues as ignoring the problem or not coming to terms with it can often lead to further and more severe health problems in the future.

To explain this a little further, I will give you a few examples. Imagine someone that is procrastinating in filing their taxes because there is a possibility that they owe money to the government. By procrastinating filling for their taxes, they are able to delay facing the possible reality that they may have to pay money, which they may or may not have. What is going on in that person's mind is that if they don't file for taxes, then they won't have to know if they owe money or not! However, the proper way to deal with a situation is to just simply do it. Even if you do hear the 'bad news' that you owe money to the government, finding out earlier will give you more time to rectify the situation rather than giving yourself no time at all. Knowing what your avoiding is only half the battle; from there, you have to take steps to correct the situation.

Cause #3: Hot-Cold Empathy Gap

In the world of psychology, there is a theory that proposes that the hot-cold empathy gap is a state of mind that causes people to underestimate how much influence their instinctive drive has on their preferences, behaviors, and attitudes. The most important aspect to understand the theory of the hot-cold empathy gap is that human understanding is heavily dependent on a person's state of mind. For instance, if a person is feeling angry, it is difficult for them to picture themselves being calm. If a person is hungry, it is hard for them to picture themselves being full.

A person's inability to minimize the empathy gap can cause numerous negative situations in professional settings. For example, imagine a doctor that is trying to get a gauge on how much pain you are feeling due to an illness. Subjective decisions, as such, are often influenced by a person's hot-cold empathy gap. If the doctor has previously experienced a similar situation as the patient, they may feel like they are overreacting to their pain, or they might be able to emphasize accurately. A person's past experiences and emotions heavily impact their decisions. Due to the fact a person's 'future self' is unknown to them, it is impossible for them to predict their emotions and mood in the future. This means that a person's future potential feelings and moods could easily disrupt their plans of accomplishing tasks. If their mood worsens, they may get into a mindset that holds them back from accomplishing the task at hand.

Cause #4: Dynamic Inconsistency

The term dynamic inconsistency is described as a situation where a person's decision-making preferences change over time, and their preferences are inconsistent. This is similar to the theory that every person has different varieties of their 'self' when they are faced with a decision. Each 'self' in a decision-making scenario represents them at a certain point in time, and when preferences are not aligned, that is when inconsistency happens. This is when unpredictability is added to that future self.

For instance, if you are studying for an exam that is happening the next day, you are probably wishing that you had one more day to study, especially if you had started studying very last minute. If you were asked that night, if you would be willing to pay $20 to postpone the exam for one more day, there is a high likelihood that you will take this offer. However, if you had been asked to pay $20 several months before the exam, you likely won't feel like you will need that extra day since you have months to prepare. Consequently, there is a high likelihood that you would not pay $20 to postpone the exam.

Although the choice is the same in both situations, since the decision is made at different points in time, you are expressing time inconsistency. This means that people often change their minds over a period of time, and the decision that they decide to make is 100% relative to when they have to make that decision. Therefore, the 'when' factor heavily influences a person's thought process. The decisions that people make vary depending on what is impacting them right now or what may impact them in the future.

Cause #5: Lack of Motivation

We lightly discussed motivation throughout this book. However, a lack of motivation is a leading cause of procrastination. We learned earlier that motivation is created AFTER doing a task and not before. Here are some of the underlying causes that may cause someone lack of motivation:

- Unclear goals
- Working in the wrong environment
- Lack of confidence
- Negative surroundings
- Past failure with this task
- Struggling with new ideas
- Other priorities
- Stress
- Fatigue
- Lack of energy

Many studies conducted surrounding a person's motivation found that people will lack motivation when they don't see value in the projected outcome of their work. On the contrary, if they were able to see clearly how their work relates and connects to their goals and interests, they are likely to feel more motivated and to value their work more. Therefore, they will have more motivation to continue investing their time and energy into it. Another similar study found that motivation is actually made up of two components; goal choice and self-confidence. They found that having self-confidence is not motivating on its own, but it acts as a judgment of a person's own abilities in regards to accomplishing their goal at hand. Therefore, self-confidence is considered to be a big part of achieving a larger conceptualization of motivation in order to achieve their set goals.

How to Overcome Procrastination

Now that we have an understanding of what the main causes of procrastination are, we are going to begin learning how to overcome it. By taking the initiative to pick up this book and begin learning about procrastination is an important first step that you have taken, so congratulate yourself on that. Simply by being aware of your own procrastination is important. In this subchapter, I will be teaching you eleven practical steps that can help you start overcoming procrastination. These steps are generally helpful for everyone; it does not require the knowledge of CBT, so you can do execute these steps without having CBT knowledge.

Step 1: Break Your Task Into Littler Tasks

As we mentioned throughout this book, one main reason that people put off doing the work that they need to do is that they subconsciously find that their work is too overwhelming for them. Start by just breaking down whatever that task is into littler parts and then focus on one at a time. If you find yourself still wanting to procrastinate after you've already broken it down, then break it down even more. You will eventually get to a point where the task that you need to do is so easy that you would feel very badly about yourself if you didn't just do it.

Let's use the tax filing example once again. Imagine that you are feeling overwhelmed as you don't even know where to begin filing your taxes. You are also afraid that you may owe money to the government that you might not have. Here is how I would break down the large and broad task of 'filing taxes':

1. Research the best way to file taxes for beginners
2. Explore my options (either downloading software for DIY or going to a tax filing company)
3. Pick which option suits you best
4. Gather the documents that are suggested based on which option you chose in step #2
5. Follow the instructions given to you by the tax software or the tax professional

Suddenly that one large task of 'filing taxes' became much more manageable. Instead of thinking about filing taxes as one large unit, you are now starting with a simple google search of the best way to file taxes for beginners. From there, now you can make an educated decision on which method is easiest for you to proceed with. By taking things one step at a time, your mind becomes less overwhelmed.

Step 2: Change Your Environment

This may be obvious to some, but different types of environments produce different impacts on a person's productivity. Take a look at your workspace, does looking at it make you want to go back to bed?

Or does it look inviting enough to make you want to jump right into work? If it's the former, you may want to consider changing up your workspace to make it more inviting. For instance, I used to have stronger feelings of procrastination when my desk was cluttered. It did not look inviting, and in fact, it added stress as now I needed to clear up my workspace before doing a task that I didn't even really want to do in the first place. By keeping your workspace clean, tidy, and inviting, you can skip the step of having to tidy up before getting your hands dirty with work.

Step 3: Create A Detailed Plan With Deadlines

When a person just has one singular deadline for a large task, it's basically an invitation to procrastinate. This is because people get under the impression that they have time and continue to keep pushing things back until the deadline is looming over them. In step one, we discussed breaking down your task into smaller ones. In this step, we will actually make our own deadlines for each small task. The purpose of this is, so you have a general idea when you have to finish each task. If you don't finish one step by the deadline that you have set, you are jeopardizing every step that's planned after that. This helps create some urgency.

Step 4: Eliminate Your Procrastination Temptations

If you are someone who is a constant procrastination offender, it may be because you make it very easy for yourself to be distracted. Be self-aware – what are the things that you typically find yourself doing when you're supposed to be doing something else? Is it browsing the internet? Scrolling your phone? Identify what exactly it is that is tempting you to procrastinate and try to prevent yourself from being tempted in the first place. If you are easily distracted by your phone, turn it off for an hour, put it in a drawer, and begin to work. Some people may extreme and go as far as disabling all their social media accounts so they can prevent themselves from endless browsing. It doesn't have to be extremely drastic, but take preventative measures, so it's not too easy for you to procrastinate.

Step 5: Surround Yourself With People Who Inspire You

Choosing who you spend your time with heavily influences your behaviors. If you are spending time with people who also procrastinate and don't see anything wrong with it, then you are likely to think that that is okay. Instead, try to surround yourself with people that are motivated and have achieved many goals before. You will soon be able to gain some of their motivation and spirit, as well.

Step 6: Get A Buddy

When you have a large set of tasks that you need to get done, having a buddy will make the process way more fun. Your buddy should ideally be someone that also has their own large set of tasks/goals that they want to complete. The two of you will hold each other accountable for the tasks that need to be done. It is not required that both of you need to have the same goals, but if they are, even better! Many people that have goals of getting more fit will likely find themselves a workout buddy that will help hold them accountable for going to the gym or even planning workout sessions together.

Step 7: Tell Others About Your Goals

This serves a similar function as the step before but on a much larger scale. Tell your friends, family, and colleagues about the goals that you have in mind. This works better if you tell them details like your deadlines or the plan that you've made for yourself. Now the next time you see these people, they will likely ask you what your status is on your goals, therefore, creating motivation for you. Also, people tend to not want to 'fail' in front of others, so if you know that you are seeing those people soon, you are more likely to make sure that you have made some progress so you can update them on it.

Step 8: Seek Out Someone Who Has Achieved Your Goal

If your goal is one that you think other people have accomplished before, try to find out who these people are. Seek them out and connect with them in order to ask them about their experience. You can learn about what obstacles and failures that they faced along the way, and they'd be able to provide you with some tips that may have made their journey a little bit easier. Moreover, seeing living proof that your goals are ones that are achievable may help you take action even sooner.

Step 9: Re-Clarify Your Goals

If you are someone that has been procrastinating for a long time now, it might be due to the misalignment of what you're currently doing and what you want. People often outgrow their goals when they begin to learn more about themselves. However, they don't always adjust their goals based on those changes. Try to take a weekend to yourself and regroup. Ask yourself, 'what exactly do I want to achieve? Are the things that I am doing now aligning with that? If not, what can I do to change it?' Adjusting your goals to something that lines up with who you are presently is crucial in terms of creating motivation and value for yourself.

Step 10: Don't Overcomplicate

This relates back to a point we talked about earlier in this book. There is never a 'perfect time' to do a task that you need to do. You may be identifying all the reasons why the present moment is 'not the best time,' but that is the wrong mindset to have. Even if you only had 10 minutes, you can surely get SOMETHING done that is related to your goal. Abandon this thought of waiting for 'the perfect time' because there will never be one. After you break down your goals into smaller ones, start doing them whenever you have 10 minutes free. It's as simple as that.

Step 11: Just Do It

At the end of it all, everything comes down to simply just taking action. Just like how we learned motivation comes from starting something and not before, just simply taking the first step to doing something will create the motivation you need to keep you going. A person can do all the planning and strategizing they need, but if they don't actually take the first step, nothing will happen.

CHAPTER 4: DISMISSING PROCRASTINATION EXCUSES

At this point in the book, you've learned about the psychology behind procrastination, the vicious cycle of procrastination, and a simple guide on how to overcome it. In this chapter, we will be taking this one step further, and I will be helping you identify what your procrastination excuses are. We will be learning some of the most common excuses that are widely used by procrastinators, testing these excuses out, and then defeating these excuses. We will end the chapter with a worksheet that will help deal with procrastination excuses.

Common Procrastination Excuses

We will start off this chapter by learning about what the most common procrastination excuses are. While you are reading through this and learning, try to see which excuses resonate with you the most. By recognizing which excuses you use most often, we can proceed to test out whether those excuses are true, or if they are simply just excuses. By proving to yourself whether or not they are true, you have a strong reason to defeat and overcome your excuses. Let's jump right in.

Excuse #1: "I will do it tomorrow."

This excuse usually appears during a person's childhood. However, a large number of adults use this excuse on a daily basis. There is an old saying that goes, "never put off till tomorrow what you can do today." Unfortunately, this saying does not stand up well in the face of the temptation of instant gratification. Instead of resisting temptation, try to think of it in a way where you're doing yourself a favor. Promise yourself some type of reward (e.g., getting your favorite take out or drawing yourself a nice bath) if you do that required task today instead of 'tomorrow.'

Excuse #2: "I don't have enough time to do this right now."

The people who rely on this excuse the most are busy professionals. They never feel like they are using an excuse because it is true that they are actually always busy. If someone is constantly on the go and completing tasks but still never getting to the end of their to-do list, it may feel natural to think that you don't have time for whatever task you promised yourself you would do. However, there is a huge flaw in this type of mindset. There will always be time to work on something; you just have to make room for it. We talked about how you can do a lot in 10 minutes of time. Simply just set aside 10 minutes of time in the morning or right before bed. That is really all you need. You'll then start to make gradual progress without the need to interfere with your daily schedule.

Excuse #3: "This is too hard to do right now."

We talked about the concept of having a large task a lot throughout this book. People that set themselves up for large tasks without making a plan often fall victim to this excuse. When a person looks at a huge set of tasks, all they can see is how big and overwhelming that one entity is. When all you're thinking about is how big that workload is, it's almost natural that you would want to avoid it for as long as possible. Rather than looking at your one large task as a monstrous unit, break it down into smaller chunks. We already talked about this, but by breaking down your task into smaller ones and focusing on those smaller ones individually, you are giving yourself an in that feels much less intimidating.

Excuse #4: "Once I finish X, I'll start working on Y."

When a person has two competing tasks or goals, inevitably, one will take a backseat. It is important to have more than one priority, but dividing your attention entirely is not the ideal way to confront this. For instance, let's say that you are working on two projects that have the same deadline at the end of the week. By the end of your first day working, you've already made a huge impact on project A, but you don't want to start project B because you don't want to shift gears. In order to not make the excuse to put off project B, start doing some preliminary tasks that project B requires in the background. You can take short 5-minute breaks from project A just to make a plan for project B. This way, when you complete project A, you already have a whole plan mapped out for project B, and you can get your feet wet right away without losing momentum.

Excuse #5: "This task is too important; it requires my full attention."

The most common victims to fall into this excuse are your nervous professionals. For instance, let's pretend that there is a huge project that's been neglected for a while, but there are a ton of your daily tasks that you still need to complete. If you truly believe that your project is the most important thing right now, you may decide to do it at a time where you aren't distracted by other trivial tasks. It does sort of make sense on one hand when it comes to a person doing their best work when they have minimal distractions. However, there will never be a time where there are no distractions. People will always have interference, and just like what we learned earlier, there is no 'perfect' time to do something. Rather than saying now is not the best time to work on it, break it down into smaller tasks and just do one of them amidst your other tasks.

Excuse #6: "It's not important enough."

This excuse comes in multiple forms. The first form of it is that you believe that this task should not even be your responsibility in the first place. For instance, your manager could have given you a task that generally isn't your responsibility. In this scenario, you may be procrastinating because you resent the fact that you got extra work. If there is an opening for you to negotiate with your boss about this task, then, by all means, go for it. However, if you know that there is no getting out of it, you might as well start sooner rather than later. Secondly, a task that you deem not important enough maybe something that is of a preventative or routine measure. These tasks tend to take a backseat in comparison to more urgent tasks, but they are also often swept under the rug when a person thinks they are insignificant. If you find yourself thinking that certain tasks just 'aren't important enough,' remind yourself that routine upkeep tasks prevent large problems in the future. If we use dental cleaning as an example, it's a lot cheaper to just get your routine checkup and cleaning every year rather than putting it off and having to do costly dental work when something does happen to you.

Excuse #7: "I'm too tired (or stressed, sad, angry…etc.)"

This excuse is probably the most used, common, and tempting one of them all. If a person finds themselves in a negative mood, all they want to do is to stop working and do something that will make them feel better. This could be just sitting at home relaxing or going out for a beer. This results in the person rationalizing with themselves that their work would be done faster and with more productivity if they try to attempt it when they are feeling better. There are two important aspects to note here. First of all, it is impossible to tell what kind of mood someone will be in the future. For all we know, this person could be in the same exact mood tomorrow and fall into the same excuse, like some sort of unproductive loop. Secondly, this is not a common thought, but working through a hard task can actually enhance someone's mood. The feeling of achievement and satisfaction that comes with finishing a task, no matter how pleasant or unpleasant, often lifts people out of a bad mood. Especially if they can get a reward after that, they feel like they deserved it.

Testing Your Excuses

Now that you know what the most common excuses are, which ones do you feel like you use most often? When you know which excuses you use most frequently, you can begin to test them to see if these excuses have any truth in them. For example, I am a constant offender of using the "I'm too tired" excuse. Although it is true that I am often tired due to long hours of writing, I need to test my excuse of whether or not I am too tired to do a required task that I need to do. In this scenario, I would ask myself, "Am I really too tired to write one more chapter?" and then "Am I too tired to watch TV or scroll on social media?" Almost 9 times out of 10, my answer is no; I am not too tired to watch TV or browse the web. Therefore, my excuse of "I'm too tired" is a lie, and I do have the energy to do some work.

Try testing your most common excuses by asking yourself these questions below, based on which excuse you find yourself using.

Your Excuse	Questions to Ask Yourself in Order to Test Said Excuse
"I will do it tomorrow."	• What is my schedule like tomorrow? • Do I actually have more time tomorrow? • What are the reasons why I can't do this task right now? (If you don't have any reasons, just get started!)
"I don't have enough time to do this right now."	• How much time do I have? (If you have at least 10 minutes, you have time) • What smaller tasks can I do in a short amount of time?
"This is too hard to do right now."	• Why is it 'too hard'? Is it because the tasks itself are too large? (If so, break down the task into smaller ones) • Will this task be too hard tomorrow? (If yes, then it's not a matter of time, it's a matter of breaking your tasks down properly) • What will make this task easier to do right now?
"Once I finish X, I'll start working on Y."	• Is there nothing I can do

	between finishing X and starting Y that will make my tasks easier? • Can I at least start a plan for task Y? • What is the likelihood that I will be able to simply dive into Y after I'm done X? (If it's a low likelihood, start some of task Y before you are finished task X)
"This task is too important; it requires my full attention."	• Is there going to ever be a time where my attention is 100% undivided? (If no, this time is as good as any)
"It's not important enough."	• What else is more important right now? • Why do I think this is not important enough? • If I neglect this now, will it catch up to me later? (If yes, then just do it right now)
"I'm too tired (or stressed, sad, angry…etc.)."	• Am I going to be less tired (or any other negative emotion) tomorrow? • How will I know for a fact that I will be feeling better tomorrow? • Can anyone know how they are going to be feeling in the future?

Defeating These Excuses

In the chart above, I provided you with a few questions to test your own excuse based on which excuses you use most often. These questions are here to show you that most of the time, your excuses are simply just excuses and that they don't hold any truth to them. Once you are aware of the fact that your excuses are empty, you can start to defeat and overcome them by simply just doing the task that you are trying to put off. The only way to overcome procrastination or excuses, in general, is to simply just take action.

Here is a procrastination excuse worksheet to help you practice overcoming your own excuses.

Worksheet #4.1 Sentence Completion Worksheet

1. If I start to feel fear regarding starting a new task, I will acknowledge that I'm probably anticipating embarrassment (or any other negative emotions) about...

_____
_____
_____
_____
_____
_____
_____
_____
_____
_____

2. When considering whether my goals are "worth it", I will say...

_____
_____
_____
_____
_____
_____
_____
_____
_____
_____

3. When I let potential fear or embarrassment get in the way of completing tasks, I will ask myself these follow question to help minimize those emotions…

4. If I feel uncertain about doing a task, and I feel like I'm on the verge of making an excuse, I will resolve this by doing…

5. I know I have the ability to work towards my goals while also honoring my daily responsibilities by making these changes to my prioritization and time management…

6. Striving for these big goals that I have will help better me in different aspects of my life in these following ways…

CHAPTER 5: CBT TECHNIQUES TO STOP PROCRASTINATION

In this chapter, we are diving into the technical techniques of CBT in order to overcome procrastination. Just to refresh our memory, we learned earlier in this book that CBT is built on a foundation of three cornerstones; cognition (thoughts), emotions (feelings), and behavior. The premise of CBT is that what a person is thinking influences their emotions, which then influences their behavior. The theory behind this is that if a person is able to control their thoughts and manage their unhelpful thinking patterns, then they would ultimately be able to control their emotions and behaviors.

Using CBT to Be Mindful of Your Thoughts

Since procrastination is mostly made up of a person's unhelpful thinking styles, CBT is a great technique to challenge this because it revolves around monitoring one's own thoughts. The first step to using CBT to manage your procrastination is to simply just try to be more aware of what you're thinking. Due to our fast-paced society that is built up of thousands of decisions a day, many people go through their daily lives on auto-pilot in order to minimize the number of decisions they have to make. They do this to preserve their energy as making that many conscious decisions every day is exhausting. If this is your first time practicing CBT, all I am asking you to do is just to try to be mindful of your thoughts. Find moments of peace and quiet, and just pay attention to what's going on in your mind. Are you letting yourself be in the present moment, or do you think about the hundreds of things that you need to get done this week?

Once you have practiced this a little bit, we will begin learning about unhelpful thinking patterns and styles. People who procrastinate often have adopted numerous unhelpful thinking styles, which makes them feel like certain tasks are extremely daunting. Combining your newly found mindfulness with unhelpful thinking styles, you will soon be able to identify when you are exercising those unhelpful thinking styles.

Unhelpful Thinking Styles

Like we just mentioned, for a person to use CBT effectively, they must understand the different types of unhelpful thinking styles or otherwise known as cognitive distortions. By understanding what these different styles are, you will be able to identify when you are exercising those styles and use CBT to interrupt those patterns and to alter your own thought process. By determining whether or not the negative emotions you are feeling are justified or not, you will then be able to control it in order to keep your mind focused on the task at hand. Below are twelve unhelpful thinking styles that people regularly exhibit:

1. All or nothing thinking: This is also commonly known as 'black and white thinking.' This type of unhealthy thinking style is when a person tends to see things in either black or white, success or failure. If their performance is not perfect, they see it as a failure.
2. Overgeneralization: This is when a person sees one single negative situation as a pattern that is never-ending. They draw conclusions of future situations based on one single event.
3. Mental filter: This is when a person chooses one single undesirable detail and exclusively dwells on it. Their perception of reality becomes negative based on that detail. They only notice their failures, but they don't see their successes.
4. Disqualifying the positive: This is when a person discounts their positive experiences or past success by saying, "that doesn't count." By discounting all positive experiences, a

person maintains a negative perspective even if it contradicts their reality.
5. Jumping to conclusions: This is when a person makes negative assumptions even when they do not have supporting evidence. There are two types of jumping to conclusions:
    a. Mind reading: The person imagines that they already know that people are thinking negatively about them, and therefore they don't bother to ask.
    b. Fortune-telling: The person predicts that things will end up badly, and they convince themselves that their prediction is a fact.
6. Magnification/Minimization: This is when a person blows things out of proportion or inappropriately shrinks something to make it seem unimportant. For instance, they may beef up somebody else's achievement (magnification) and shrug off their own achievements (minimization).
7. Catastrophizing This is when a person associates terrible and extreme consequences to the outcome of situations and events. For instance, if they are rejected for a date, they take that as being alone forever.
8. Emotional reasoning: This is when a person makes the assumption that their negative emotions are reflective of reality. For instance, "I feel that it is this way; therefore, it is true."
9. "Should" statements: This is when a person motivates themselves by using "shoulds" and "shouldn'ts" as if they associate rewards and punishments with every task they do. Since they associate rewards with shoulds and punishment with shouldn'ts, when other people don't follow their 'should' statements, they may feel angry or frustrated.
10. Labeling and mislabeling: This is when a person overgeneralizes to the extreme. Rather than describing their mistake, they automatically give themselves a negative label, such as "I'm a loser." They also do this to others; if someone else's behavior is undesirable, they label them as a "loser" as well.
11. Personalization: This is when a person takes responsibility for something that wasn't their fault. They see themselves as the cause of an external situation.

12. All at once bias: This is when a person thinks that risks and threats are right at their front step, and the amount of it is increasing. When these thoughts occur, they tend to:
    a. Think that negative situations are evolving faster than they can come up with solutions.
    b. Think that certain situations are moving too quickly, and they feel overwhelmed.
    c. Think that there is no time to do anything between now and the oncoming threat.
    d. Numerous risks and threats seem to all appear at the same time.

Identifying Your Own Unhelpful Thinking Patterns

When it comes to procrastination, procrastinators tend to foster the following unhelpful thinking patterns:
- All or nothing thinking
- Overgeneralization
- Mental filter
- Disqualifying the positive
- Jumping to conclusions (fortune-telling)
- Catastrophizing
- Emotional Reasoning

Now that you have an understanding of every single unhelpful thinking style try to identify which one you exhibit the most. For example, I often fall victim to perfectionism. When I feel like something isn't done 100% correctly, I am convinced that I have failed. I fail to see that there isn't such thing as 'perfect' and that a not 'perfect' score can still be a good score. This type of thinking style makes me afraid to take on new things or go after my goals because if the trajectory of my journey is not "perfect," I will feel like that it was an utter failure.

Try to think about your own thought processes and how you tend to read your own thoughts. You may need to take a few weeks in this process as being able to identify your own thinking patterns comes from being mindful of your own thoughts, to begin with. Once you have an idea of what your unhelpful thinking styles are, we will move on to learning about how to challenge them. Don't rush this step, as this is crucial.

Challenging Your Unhelpful Thinking Styles

Once you are able to identify what your unhelpful thinking styles are, you can begin to challenge them in order to reshape those thoughts into something that is more factual and realistic. In this subchapter, I have categorized all the different types of unhealthy thinking styles for you and question that you should be asking yourself when you catch yourself having those thoughts.

Keep in mind that reshaping thought processes that were developed through decades of habits is not an easy task. It requires a lot of effort and dedication to change our own thoughts, so don't get frustrated if you are not finding success right away. Whenever you feel like you are getting stuck, just simply fall back on the first step, mindfulness. Simply just paying attention to your thoughts more often will make CBT easier for you.

Probability Overestimation
If you are someone that is finding that your thoughts are often made up of possible negative outcomes, you may be a victim to probability overestimation. This is where a person overestimates the probability of failure or something bad happening. Try to ask yourself these questions below in order to reevaluate your thoughts:
- From my experience, what is the probability that this thought will actually come true?
- What are the other possible results that could arise from this situation? Is the outcome that I am thinking of now the only possibility? Does my feared outcome have the highest probability compared to the other outcomes?
- Have I ever experienced this type of situation before? If so, what happened? What have I learned from these past experiences that would be helpful to me now?
- If a friend or loved one is having these negative thoughts, what would I say to them?

Catastrophizing
- If the prediction that I am fearful of really did come true, how bad would it really be?
- If I am feeling embarrassed, how long will this last? How long will others realistically remember it? What are all the different things they could be saying/thinking? IS it 100% that they will only talk about the negative things?
- I am feeling uncomfortable at the moment, but is this really that horrible of an outcome?
- What are the other alternatives for how this situation could turn out?
- If a loved one was having the same thoughts as me, what would I say to them?

Mind Reading
- Is it really possible that I know what other people are thinking? What are the other possible things that they could be thinking about that's unrelated to me?
- Do I have evidence to support my own assumptions?
- In the scenario that my assumptions are true, what is so bad about it?

Personalization
- What other elements might be playing a role in the situation? Could it be the other person's stress, deadlines, or mood?
- Does somebody always have to be at blame?
- A conversation is never just one person's responsibility.
- Were any of these circumstances out of my control?

Should Statements
- Would I be holding the same standards to a loved one or a friend?
- Are there any exceptions?
- Will someone else does this differently?

All or Nothing Thinking
- Is there a middle ground or a grey area that I am not

considering?
- Would I judge a friend or loved one in the same way?
- Was the entire situation 100% negative? Was there any part of the situation that I handled well?
- Is having/showing some anxiety such a horrible thing?

Selective Attention/Memory
- What are the positive elements of the situation? Am I ignoring those?
- Would a different person see this situation differently?
- What strengths do I have? Am I ignoring those?

Negative Core Beliefs
- Do I have any evidence that supports my negative beliefs?
- Is this thought true in every situation?
- Would a loved one or friend agree with my self-belief?

Chronic procrastinators often are stuck in their own unhelpful thinking styles that cause them to prioritize other things rather than the most important ones to them. By fixing their own unhelpful thinking styles, they will be able to change their thought process to one that is more productive and adds more value to achieving their goals.

I have provided you a couple of CBT practice worksheets that aim to help you identify your own unhelpful thinking styles and to help you challenge them in order to overcome your own procrastination.

Worksheet #5.1 Dysfunctional Thought Record

This worksheet aims to help people who struggle with their own negative thoughts that lead them to exhibit undesirable behavior. This is also great for the people that are looking to figure out when these thoughts typically occur (e.g. an hour before you're supposed to do said task? Two hours before? A day before?) By learning about what types of events trigger your unhealthy thinking styles, it makes it easier to address and to build new ones.

This worksheet is made of a chart that is divided into seven columns:
1. The far left of this chart will be used for you to write down the date and time of when exactly your dysfunctional thought arose. (e.g., Did these unhealthy thoughts arise an hour before you're supposed to complete a task? Two hours before? A day before?)
2. The second column is where you will write down the situation that leads up to your unhelpful thoughts. Describe the events that led up to them.
3. The third column is where you write down what your automatic thoughts were. This is where you will record your automatic thought and rate if with how much you believe it from 0 – 100.
4. The fourth column is where you will write the emotions that arose due to your thoughts. Rate how strongly you feel them from 0 – 100.
5. The fifth column is 'cognitive distortion.' This is where you will write down which unhelpful thinking styles you are exhibiting. Refer back to the list of unhelpful thinking styles if you need help with identifying which ones you have.
6. The sixth column is where you will write down what alternative thoughts you'd rather have. Try thinking of more positive and helpful thoughts in order to replace the negative ones.
7. The last column is where you will write down the outcome after doing this worksheet. Answer questions like "Did you write down an alternative thought that was convincing yet positive?" or "were you able to identify and confront the dysfunctional thought?" or "Were you able to lower your beliefs in those negative thoughts?"

Date & Time When did this thought occur?			
Situation What was the context? What other things were happening at the time and before the thought?			
Automatic Thought Describe your thought and rate how much you believed it between 0 - 100.			
Emotion What feelings arose at this time? What was its intensity from 0-100?			
Cognitive Distortion E.g. Catastrophizing, filtering, personalization...etc.			
Alternative Thoughts What is a more realistic and positive thought?			
Outcome Re-rate how much you believe the original thought and emotions from 0 - 100.			

Worksheet #5.2 Cognitive Restructuring

This exercise uses questioning as a technique to help the individual challenge illogical or irrational thoughts. This is particularly helpful when someone is looking to overcome procrastination as most of the time, their reasoning for doing something is illogical.

The top of this chart describes how one's thoughts are a continuous mental narrative. Due to the fleeting nature of it, we don't often get an opportunity to challenge these thoughts. This exercise aims to help us identify a few of these thoughts, so we are able to analyze them.

1. The first section of this chart is "What I am thinking" this is where the individual will write down one specific thought that they think is dysfunctional or irrational.
2. Then, they will write down the supporting evidence for and against that thought. What proof is there that this is true? What proof is there that it is not true?
3. Next, they can make a final judgment on this thought. Specifically, determine whether this thought is founded on evidence or opinion.

What I am thinking:

Facts Supporting the Thought	Facts Contradicting the Thought
• _____	• _____
• _____	• _____
• _____	• _____
• _____	• _____
• _____	• _____
• _____	• _____
• _____	• _____
• _____	• _____
• _____	• _____
• _____	
• _____	• _____

Is thought based on evidence or opinion?

CHAPTER 6: CHALLENGES OF OVERCOMING PROCRASTINATION

At this point in the book, you should have a very good understanding of procrastination, the nature of it, cognitive behavioral therapy, and how to use CBT to combat the unhealthy thinking styles that cause procrastination. In this chapter, we will be learning the challenges that people will face during their journey of overcoming procrastination. Most of these challenges exist within ourselves, and we have to learn how to tolerate the discomfort of challenging our own thoughts. Thankfully, you are already on the right track if you have finished the CBT chapter! In this chapter, we will be learning about three main challenges that come with overcoming procrastination.

- Your inner-critic
- Breaking out of bad habits
- Changing your unhelpful thinking styles

The main challenge that we will focus on in this chapter is your inner-critic, as that is the one that typically prevents people from doing the things that they truly want to do. We already have a good idea of the role that unhelpful thinking styles play in a procrastinator. We will also learn a little about bad habits that people develop over the years and how people can practice self-discipline in order to overcome bad habits and learn good ones.

Your Inner-Critic

A person's inner-critic plays a huge role when it comes to things like mental health, self-esteem, and in our case, procrastination. We notice that our inner-critics usually live in a world that is black and white, a world with very little room for grey areas. Inner-critics share words with you, such as, "You should just give up." Or "What makes you think you'll succeed?" Instead of creating an open space that allows for mistakes, growth, and development, our inner-critics cause us to question our worth, which makes it difficult for us to have the right mindset to complete needed tasks.

For some people, their inner-critic is reflective of a voice from their past. It could be their mother, father, the boss that fired you. For others, it could simply be your own voice talking down at you. Often times, anybody who makes an offhand comment at you may cause you to take it so deeply that those words become a part of your identity.

This is why mindfulness is very important when we are looking to overcome procrastination by training our inner-critic. Mindfulness helps people see their own negative thoughts that are said to themselves in a repetitive cycle of self-detriment. When we continue to judge ourselves harshly, we may think that we are making progress in terms of improving our flaws when, in reality, we are only reinforcing the feelings of unworthiness.

In our world today, it is a cultural norm to believe that self-criticism will bring motivation to achieving goals and avoiding procrastination. This type of self-criticism functions under the false belief that when a person realizes that their actions or performance isn't good enough, they'll want to change. Our inner-critic is also guilty for giving us a sense of control, but not in the right places. We also use our own judgmental thoughts as a way of coping with emotions like shame, fear, and the unknown. Over time, these comments made by yourself or other people manifest inside of you and eventually become your own unique "inner-critic." To put it in its simplest form, your inner-critic is the persistent negative self-talk that keeps us stuck.

Unfortunately, the type of communication that our inner-critic uses with us are very anxiety-provoking and shaming, which actually creates something that is the complete opposite of motivation. It triggers us to stay safe, reduce anxiety, and to avoid. Avoidance with the goal of reducing anxiety is not the same as having the motivation to change.

In fact, avoidance is usually made up of things like procrastination, addictive behaviors, or self-distracting behaviors (constantly checking your phone, excessively browsing the web). If the messages that our inner-critic is telling us are often shameful, such as "why are you so lazy?" or "what's wrong with you?" we often become paralyzed. When people feel shame, they feel that there is something that is so flawed within them that they don't feel worthy of connections with other people. Shame is the emotion that disconnects us from other people and teaches us to feel alone. As humans, it is within our nature to crave a certain level of human connection. When we often feel feelings of shame caused by our inner-critic, these feelings make us want to withdraw from the world and further trigger avoidance behaviors like procrastination as a way to soothe or comfort ourselves. Ultimately, shame and self-criticism work hand in hand to prevent us from doing the things that we need to do in order to reach our goals or simply just to take care of ourselves.

Similar to CBT, awareness is the first step that needs to be taken in order to recognize your inner-critic and to reshape it into something that is less critical and more supportive. Try to pay attention the next time you are feeling distracted, numb, or anxious. Try to identify whose voice is the voice of your inner-critic. Try to find the situation where your inner-critic awakens. Allow yourself to dig deep and identify the most vulnerable feelings during situations where your inner-critic is awake. These feelings or these situations are likely what your inner-critic is trying to protect you from feeling. However, by protecting you, they are holding you back from meeting your full potential.

Here is an example of a person's inner-critic in action:

Caitlin went shopping over the weekend. She hasn't gone in a while and is unsure about her sizes at this one store, and she tried on a few items. She thought to herself, "These pants are too tight, they don't fit, I feel so fat, ugly, and unattractive. I am such a failure."

What is Caitlin afraid of exactly? Her thought process is this: "I've gained weight, which means that I failed. It also means that I'm old, and I am scared of aging and gaining even more weight."

What are Caitlin's vulnerabilities in this case?

Caitlin responds why "I feel that I don't have any control and that I am afraid. My body is functioning differently than it used to, and I'm having a harder time maintaining a healthy weight and muscle tone. I feel like this is hopeless. I feel overwhelmed and scared."

What does Caitlin really need to do in this situation?

Caitlin says, "I can deal with this change. By acknowledging my vulnerability, it causes me to make more effort to take better care of my physical health. When I feel worthless, I am unproductive. Shaming myself is not motivating."

A person's inner-critic may say negative things to you, but its true intention is to prevent you from harm by demotivating you from doing things that may result in failure in order to prevent you from feeling negative emotions. For example, Caitlin's inner-critic may be telling her that she's a failure and overweight in order to prevent her from taking better care of her body. From doing this, Caitlin will be demotivated by working out at the gym or eating healthier. If she doesn't do this, she will not fail. This is what the inner-critic is trying to do. By demotivating the person to a point where they'd rather not try is the safest protection of them all, if you don't try, you can't exactly fail.

In the later parts of this chapter, we will be doing a few worksheets that will help to recognize your inner-critic, questioning it, and training it to be more helpful rather than critical.

Breaking Out of Bad Habits

Humans are creatures of their own habit. You may know from your own experience that you don't like straying away from your existing habits and routines. It feels uncomfortable. Humans tend to find comfort in old habits and routines. Unfortunately, a lot of the times our habits are not positive ones. Most people tend to have bad habits such as indulging in the conveniences of junk food, drinking alcohol every night, or skipping the gym for an extra hour of sleep. If you have a couple of bad habits yourself, you may know very well that the urge to act out these habits is very strong. However, there is a silver lining to this. If bad habits can be so strong and tempting, it means that good habits can be like that too. It all comes down to a matter of incorporating those good habits in your life and ingraining it so deeply that it feels wrong or uncomfortable to not act out those habits.

So, where exactly do our habits come from, and how are they developed? Why is it that when people try to change their habits by breaking out of bad ones and building good ones that they can only stick with it for a short amount of time before they give up and revert to their old ways? The biggest problem here is that the bad habits we have are likely the habits that we've had for many years and maybe even decades. Our habits are made up of neural pathways that have been imprinted into our brains. This is something that happens on a biological level. These neural pathways are responsible for linking up the neural networks in a person's brain to perform specific functions like pouring a cup of coffee in a certain way, smoking a cigarette, or walking up the stairs.

These neural pathways help a person automate certain behaviors that are constantly used in order to reduce the energy needed for the conscious processing power in a person's brain. By automating certain actions, it allows this person's mind to focus on other things rather than the mundane tasks that they have done a thousand times. This function actually stems from our very early human days and is actually a part of our DNA. This function allows us to have a more efficient mind that can be used for many things and not just entirely focused on simply daily tasks.

It is often the mundane behaviors that are repeated, which then holds people back from being able to build good habits. Most of the time, people tend to have more bad habits that add negative value to their lives rather than good habits that help them reach their goals further. Since neural pathways get ingrained deeper and deeper over time, it makes it difficult for people to break out of their bad habits or form good ones when they are constantly acting out on bad habits.

Unhelpful Thinking Styles

We talked about unhelpful thinking styles a lot in the previous chapter. This is one of the biggest challenges that people face when they are looking to overcome procrastination. The difficulty comes from first being able to be aware of your own thoughts and then paying attention to what types of patterns your thoughts occur in. When a person is able to recognize when those thinking styles are happening, that's when they can begin to interrupt them, challenge them, and change them.

For instance, let's say you need to hand in a report to your boss the next weekend. You know for a fact that it will take you several hours and that you have a jam-packed week coming up. You're sitting at home, and your thoughts begin to mindlessly wander. You begin to think that this report is too hard (although you haven't started yet) and that you are going to fail. You begin to feel stressed and anxious, and then you say to yourself "I'm too stressed right now to do this report. I'll start on it tomorrow." We learned in the previous chapter that there are multiple things wrong here. Firstly, since you were mindless when thinking about the report, you looked at the report as one giant hard task. That is the first mistake. The second mistake here is letting that one giant report cause emotions of stress and anxiety, which led you to "feel too stressed" to start the report right now. The third mistake is saying to yourself, "I'll start on it tomorrow," as you fully know that the rest of your week will be very busy.

CBT becomes useful here because if you were being mindful of your current thoughts, rather than exhibiting the jumping to conclusions unhelpful thinking style, you would be able to catch yourself thinking that the report is too difficult before even tried. If you were able to stop yourself there and take a few steps back and instead think "I believe this report is a big project so, in order to make it easier for myself, I have to break it down into smaller and more manageable pieces." By doing this, you likely will not end up feeling those emotions of anxiety and stress, which then led to procrastination. Do you see how simply just being aware of your thoughts and challenging yourself can change the outcome of a situation entirely?

When a person learns to be able to tolerate the discomfort of challenging their own thoughts, they can overcome bad habits and things that they never thought they were going to be able to. It may sound easy, but it requires a lot of practice for a person to be able to start paying attention to thoughts that they have ignored for years. So the next time you feel like you're about to procrastinate doing something, just pay attention to the emotions you're feeling. Work backward. Ask yourself, 'why am I feeling these emotions right now?" "what triggered these emotions" "if ABC trigged these emotions, what can I do to make it more manageable?"

Learning About Your Inner-Critic

Now that we have learned how to use CBT to begin challenging our own thoughts in order to overcome bad procrastination habits, we will now be taking it one step further and challenging our inner-critic. We learned that our inner-critic often is a voice within us that normally does not tell us the most encouraging things. In fact, this voice often takes on the form of someone who has criticized you in the past. It could be a parent, significant other, good friend, or even just a stranger. Our inner-critic's purpose is to protect us from harm, although it's words and actions may be responsible for producing more harm. In this subchapter, we will be learning how to question, acknowledge, and train your inner-critic to be more helpful and supportive rather than critical.

Question Your Inner-Critic

Questioning your inner-critic is something that requires a little bit of CBT technique. CBT here works by helping you acknowledge thoughts that you would normally just subconsciously absorb but not actually be aware of. For example, if an individual finds themselves feeling 'useless' in a certain situation, if they paid attention and became aware of these unhelpful thoughts, they can begin to question their inner-critic who called them 'useless.' They can start by asking, "What evidence is there that supports the accusation that I am a loser?" and "What evidence is there that doesn't support the accusation that I am a loser?" When people start asking themselves these questions, they often find that they aren't much or any evidence at all that supports the negative statements that their inner-critic is saying about them. The ability to catch themselves thinking thoughts that don't have support evidence is a sign that you have learned to question your inner-critic.

We will now be focusing on learning to catch the moments where our inner-critic begins to say negative things about us and then find a way to contradict those statements. Before we begin, below is a list of responses that you can say in response to your inner-critic.

1) Stop saying the same unhelpful negative statements about me. I have supporting evidence that I am not the things you are describing me as. I will change you into a voice that will tell me more encouraging things instead.
2) You are lying. I have evidence that does not support the statements you are saying about me. By taking an objective look at myself, I found that I am not the things that you are saying about me.
3) I belong. You are mimicking the voice of bullies in my childhood, and your words hold no truth. I have grown up to be a good and respectful person.
4) I am not weak. I have faced and conquered many of my fears, and I plan on continuing to do so. Your words do not have any supporting evidence.
5) I am not afraid. I have faced many of my fears head-on and conquered them. I will continue to do this.
6) Stop beating me up. Stop hurting my motivation and inspiration because I don't want to have more negative thoughts. I will replace your negative words with positive ones about myself and my goals.

Worksheet #6.1 Training Your Inner-Critic (Four-Step Guide)

Step 1: Revive Your Curiosity

The first step that comes with training your inner-critic is to just simply start being aware of it. In order to do this, you will need to be curious. Most people in our modern-day society moves through life in a passive manner. Due to how fast-paced society has become, people no longer give their feelings and thoughts the attention that it needs, and due to this, we tend to forget about them. Although people feel a multitude of emotions on a daily basis, they don't acknowledge these feelings every single time. Instead, people have learned to just react to things on auto-pilot. When people function this way, they don't learn to question or evaluate the downsides to the decisions and actions that we are making.

For most people, living on auto-pilot is the easiest option. Due to the immense number of decisions that people need to make in a day, living on auto-pilot means that they can make a good chunk of decisions. People have learned to just accept things as the way they are, even if they disagree or don't like it. People would rather not spend their energy or effort into changing things. It's just simply easier to leave things as it is. However, if you are reading this book right now, I think it's safe for me to assume that you are looking to change your life and are not happy with where you are at right now. By reading this book, you are actively making a decision to take matters into your own hands to improve all your bad habits and thought patterns in order to beat procrastination. The first step that you need to take in this guide is to simply just be more curious about the thoughts that are happening in your mind. Try to ignite some curiosity regarding your emotional experiences and pay attention to the way that you are speaking to yourself when you are in a difficult situation or if you are approached by a challenge. This may sound simple, but acknowledging your passive thoughts is actually very difficult since we are very used to living on auto-pilot. The human mind automatically filters out certain things due to helping you save energy and the fact that it knows that those things may upset you.

Here is the first exercise in this process. There is a list of questions below that you will use to practice questioning your inner-critic. You can either do this exercise in planned sessions, or you can keep these questions close to you to ask your inner-critic when it awakens. This decision is entirely up to you, but the more often you do this exercise, the more effective the later exercises will be.

1. What is my Inner-critic saying to me?

A:_____

2. What is my Inner-Critic saying about me specifically?

A:_____

3. When does my Inner-Critic say these things? Be as specific as possible.

A:_____

_____
_____
_____
_____
_____
_____

4. As a result of those things, what do I normally think about myself?

A:_____
_____
_____
_____
_____
_____
_____
_____
_____

5. What are the common patterns and themes that I recognize regarding my inner-critic?

A:_____
_____
_____
_____
_____
_____
_____
_____
_____
_____

6. How do all these things together affect my overall behavior?

A:_____
_____
_____

7. What do all these thoughts say about me?
A:

8. Where do these opinions come from?
A:

9. Are these opinions factual, or are they all made up?
A:

10. Is it even appropriate to think this way in this certain situation?
A:_____

11. Where/when did I start learning to think this way?
A:_____

12. Are there any childhood experiences that stand out to me? Do I think that these experiences have an effect on the way I think now?
A:_____

13. Is there anybody that may have instilled these thoughts into my mind?

A:_____

14. Does this type of thinking even make sense, logically?

A:_____

By answering the question above, you are helping yourself analyze your thought progression and figure out what role they play during real-life situations. You should now be able to see clearly the relationship between your past relationships and how it's affecting your behavior presently.

Step 2: Acknowledge Your Inner-critic

In order to prevent falling back into old habits of letting your inner-critic speak to you however it wants, we will practice acknowledging it instead. People often try to resist thinking about a certain topic, but it usually ends up with them thinking about it more and having it affect them even more largely. Rather than resisting the words that the inner-critic speaks, try to acknowledge them instead. Shift your mindset in order to see your inner-critic's words as opinions and concerns for your well-being instead of taking them as insults. Try to believe that your inner-critic has their best intentions for you and is trying to help you, just in a very misguided way. Although the inner-critic may be hindering you now, its intentions come from a place of care. In this exercise, start having a conversation with your inner-critic and ask them the follow questions. Write your answers in the lines below.

1. What is my inner-critic trying to protect me from?

A:_____
_____
_____
_____
_____
_____
_____
_____
_____
_____

2. What does my inner-critic not want me to feel or experience?

A:_____
_____
_____

_____
_____
_____
_____
_____
_____
_____
_____

3. Why is this important to my inner-critic?

A:_____
_____
_____
_____
_____
_____
_____
_____
_____
_____

4. Are the words my inner-critic is using critical or constructive?

A:_____
_____
_____
_____
_____
_____
_____
_____
_____
_____

5. Are the words being used designed to help me improve or to criticize me?

A:_____
_____

_____
_____
_____
_____
_____
_____
_____
_____

6. Are the words being used based on factual evidence? Or are they based on an opinion?

A:_____
_____
_____
_____
_____
_____
_____
_____
_____

7. If I take these words into consideration, where in my life might I need to make some changes?

A:_____
_____
_____
_____
_____
_____
_____
_____
_____

8. How else could I make changes in my life without all this resistance from my inner-critic?

A:_____
_____
_____
_____
_____
_____
_____
_____
_____
_____
_____
_____

When you have completed this exercise, try to keep in mind when moving forward that your inner-critic will always be a part of you. It is a part of you in the same way that a worried parent or friend would want to look out for you and is trying to keep you out of harm's way. However, your inner-critic is actually very biased because it comes from a place of wanting to protect you, so their positive intentions end up holding you back from personal growth. At the end of the day, the most important part is for you to know the difference between your inner-critic's attempt at protection and your actual abilities.

Step 3: Thank and Appreciate Your Inner-Critic

In this step, we will take the opportunity to thank our inner-critic's for their constant concern and their desire to always step in and help out. Everyone's inner-critic has shared a multitude of opinions with them, and now it's time to interrupt them and change the way that they are helping into a method that is actually beneficial to you. If the things that your inner-critic is saying to you actually is justified, then you can go ahead and listen to it for guidance. However, if you feel like what its saying doesn't have justification, then you can feel quite confident about how their suggestions are empty. In this exercise, we will be thanking our inner-critic for everything that they have done until today. Please fill in the blanks below.

Dear Inner-Critic,

Thank you for always cautioning me of _____. Thank you for always watching over me in _____ situations. I appreciate all the different times that you told me that I couldn't do _____, but I want to tell you that I am capable of doing _____. Instead of telling me lies that you have heard from my childhood, or other people in my life, I want you to tell me constructive criticism such as; _____. You are always welcome to give me feedback, but if you are acting stubborn, I will ignore you.

Sincerely,

_____

Step 4: Negotiate With Your Inner-Critic

The ideal situation that you want to be in with your inner-critic is to come to a mutual understanding. Always keep in mind that the main concern of your inner-critic is your safety. They want to protect you from harm's way. Instead of simply ignoring your inner-critic, try to find a way to prove to them why the decisions and goals you are making are out of your own best interest. It is possible that your inner-critic will understand and give you some support in doing those things.

This next exercise is simple; you will be filling out the chart below. This chart functions to help you identify the things your inner-critic is saying to you and the things you can say back to negotiate with it. I have also provided you with some examples to give you a better understanding.

Your Goal	What You Expect Your Inner-Critic to Say	How You Will Negotiate With Your Inner-Critic
Ex: I want to get another college degree so I can learn a new skill that will help me get a job in that field.	*Ex: You have already been working full time for three years, by going back to college now you are admitting to others that you have failed your career. People will judge you.*	*Ex: Not everybody will like me, so judgments from others are normal. I am not happy at my current job, so starting something new is healthy for me. My happiness and wellbeing are more important than the things people might say about me.*
Ex: I hate my job right now, and I want to quit to travel the world for a few months.	*Ex: Quitting a full-time job is an irresponsible thing to do. You just want to take a long vacation. You will never accomplish anything if you quit.*	*Ex: I am not a quitter, as I have seen many things throughout my life. I don't want to keep working a dead-end job that I'm miserable in. Traveling is not the same as an extended vacation; I want to learn new things about the world.*

By the time you have finished these exercises, you should have gained more awareness regarding your inner-critic. Try to think about these exercises on a daily basis to continue boosting your awareness. By figuring out what comments your inner-critic is saying to you that prevents you from accomplishing the things you need to know, you can begin to challenge them and shape them into something that is of a more encouraging manner.

CHAPTER 7: THE POWER OF GETTING STARTED

In the last chapter of this book, we will be learning about combining everything you learned regarding CBT and your inner-critic in order to challenge your procrastination. Procrastination comes from a person's mental ability to overcome instant gratification and choose to do something that benefits their future-self rather than their present-self. However, when people have developed unhelpful thinking processes, it is hard to make decisions to benefit their future-self because their thoughts create negative emotions that drive away motivation. Our inner-critic's act in a similar way that creates procrastination. In order to prevent us from feeling hurt due to experiencing failure, our inner-critic would rather us to simply not do anything at all and only choose to do the things that we find comforting like watching TV or eating your favorite junk food. By teaching your inner-critic to let you take risks and work towards your goals that are valid, you will take away the negativity that's been driving away your motivation.

Do you see now how CBT and your inner-critic can be used to prevent procrastination by creating a natural flow of motivation? Rather than struggling to overcome procrastination every time you are faced with a decision, CBT, and challenging your inner-critic works by preventing that feeling of procrastination in the first place by completely rewiring your brain, habits, and thought processes. Some can argue that simply increasing your willpower to overcome instant gratification to make good choices is a faster solution to a procrastination problem. However, it is not a long-lasting one. As we learned, bad habits are built through many years, and no amount of willpower can handle overcoming that many bad habits in a person's life. Rewiring your brain to minimize the amount of procrastination you feel in the first place is a much more efficient method to approach this problem.

To make things easy for you, I will be providing you with a step by step guide on how to use CBT and inner-critic to help you fight procrastination. This guide will help you rewire all your thinking processes in order to minimize procrastination altogether. This way, you don't need to be exercising willpower every time you are faced with a decision, your brain will be trained to make the decision that benefits your future-self.

How to Use CBT and Your Inner-Critic to Prevent Procrastination (7 Step Guide)

This guide consists of seven steps that combine everything that you have learned thus far in this book. It is developed by studying the psychology of procrastination and using proven techniques like CBT to minimize its effects. Although the study of inner-critic is less funded compared to the research based on CBT, the concept of the inner-critic is one that is used by many psychologists.

Step 1: Mindfulness

The first step in this guide is simply to practice mindfulness. Mindfulness will be used for two components. The first is for CBT, and the second is for your inner-critic. Becoming aware of your own thoughts is the most crucial step in this entire guide, as everything else will fail without it. If you are a chronic procrastinator, it is very likely that you often function in a mindless manner. By functioning in a mindless manner, you are training your mind to feel more satisfaction when you choose tasks that produce instant gratification rather than tasks that you should be doing in order to achieve your goal.

There are many ways that a person can practice mindfulness. You could simply just sit quietly for five minutes and concentrate on the environment around you and pay attention to what thoughts are going through your mind as you are observing. Yoga is also a very effective method of practicing mindfulness, and it incorporates being mindful of your physical feelings and having the aid of a guided session. If you are a beginner at mindfulness, consider taking meditation or yoga classes to get a good foundation. Nowadays, people can also practice mindfulness but finding guided meditations online. There are plenty of apps and videos on YouTube nowadays that provide people with guided mindfulness meditations.

As a beginner, try to practice mindfulness via guided sessions. Once you get a good grip on it, you can begin to just start practicing mindfulness everywhere you go by using some of the techniques you've learned.

Step 2: Pay Attention to Your Thoughts

Pay attention to your thoughts, and whenever you feel a negative emotion, work backward. Try to figure out what thoughts were just on your mind before you felt negative emotions. Emotions that you should be looking out for are stress, anxiety, self-loathing, sadness, demotivation, anger, and frustration. These emotions are the ones that typically cause a person to choose instant gratification for comfort, which leads to procrastination.

This step is different from mindfulness as paying attention to your thoughts will help you identify what thoughts are going through your mind during an intense emotional moment. Mindfulness is simply just being aware of thoughts as they are happening even when you are not feeling emotional.

Just like how you will be paying attention to those thoughts that occurred before feeling a negative emotion, pay attention to the thoughts that occurred before feeling a positive emotion. By identifying what those thoughts were, you will begin to learn what types of thoughts bring positive emotions. Typically, when a person is feeling emotions that are positive, it creates more motivation and inspiration to reach goals. Adopting helpful thought processes fosters better emotions overall, which leads to more productive behaviors.

Step 3: Catch Your Own Unhelpful Thinking Patterns

In this step, we will focus on catching our own unhelpful thinking patterns. This step is no different than the chapter that we spent learning about the different types of unhelpful thinking styles and how to identify them. To refresh your memory, read through that chapter again and get a good understanding of each and every one of the unhelpful thinking styles. By understanding each one in-depth, you will have an easier time identifying when you are exhibiting those styles.

A few tips I can provide you to help yourself identify when you're showcasing these behaviors is to simply pay attention to when you're feeling anxious or completely demotivated. This a symptom that your mind has spiraled, leaving you to feel completely hopeless and unproductive. Often times, if the person had just paid attention to their thought process, they would be able to catch themselves before their mind automatically spiraled to a place of complete de-motivation. By catching yourself before you get there, you can prevent procrastination by not letting yourself lose inspiration.

Step 4: Challenge Your Unhelpful Thoughts With Evidence-Based Arguments

The next step in this guide is to begin challenging your unhelpful thoughts and thinking styles using evidence-based arguments. What this means is that you will be showing yourself evidence that supports or doesn't support the thoughts that are on your mind. I will explain this a little better with an example. Imagine that you are stressing about a public speaking event where you will be one of the speakers. You are procrastinating working on your speech because you are afraid that you will embarrass yourself in front of others. You are giving yourself the excuse that "I work better under pressure, and I can wing this and improvise!" However, you know deep down that it is not a good idea to improvise during a public speech. In this example, if you have been practicing the CBT methods, you would catch yourself in the act of catastrophizing. The moment that you thought "I'm going to embarrass myself in front of everyone" is when you started catastrophizing. At that point, you should use evidence-based arguments to negotiate with your own thoughts. You can think to yourself, "How many public speaking events have I done before?" or "Have I ever embarrassed myself in front of people?" or "I have embarrassed myself before, but was it really that bad?" By showing yourself evidence, you can cancel out those negative thinking styles and give yourself the confidence and motivation to overcome procrastination. If a person is stuck in the mindset of "Oh, I'm going to fail and embarrass myself anyway, so why prepare?" then they will almost 100% choose to not work on their speech and do something that comforts them instead.

Step 5: Challenge Your Inner-Critic

This step is only slightly different than the previous one. In this step, you will be actively challenging the things that your inner-critic is telling you. Your inner-critic has never been tamed before, so it is used to speaking whatever it takes to stop you from doing things that may potentially cause you harm. Unfortunately, in this world, almost everything has the potential to cause you harm. This doesn't mean that you shouldn't go out and try things just because there is a risk of getting hurt.

We learned in the previous chapter several ways that you can question, acknowledge, and challenge your inner-critic. You will be applying that to your day to day life. The voice of your inner-critic may cause similar effects to your unhelpful thinking styles. Just like the example we used above, your inner-critic may be telling you, "Back out of the public speaking event now before you make a fool of yourself!" or "You'll never be a good presenter!" When you have the ability to notice these voices and statements, simply acknowledge them and begin to negotiate with your inner-critic. Let them know that you thank them for looking out for you, but you are confident in your ability to do a good speech. You can let them know that even though you may fail and feel embarrassed, it is still better than a lifetime of holding back. Since your inner-critic is a part of you, after all, it can listen to reason as long as you allow yourself to be reasoned with.

When your inner-critic begins to tell you that you can't do a certain thing, or you're not good enough, or you're not worthy enough, simply find evidence within your past experience to challenge it. Prove to your inner-critic why they are wrong and why holding you back is only going to do more harm than if you failed whatever task you were planning to do. The more you tell your inner-critic this, the more they will learn to listen to you and help you in another way that is not just preventing you from doing things.

Step 6: Negotiate With Your Inner-Critic

In this step, we will focus on more of the details of how you can negotiate with your inner-critic. Although it sounds simple to just tell your inner-critic to be more supportive, you need to almost trick it into being on your side. Let's use our public speaking example again. If your inner-critic in that example is telling you that you're a bad public speaker or people are going to laugh at you, you need to find evidence in your experience where this is not true. You can talk to your inner-critic with a little humor such as "Sure, I have embarrassed myself before, but I'd rather be embarrassed than repressed forever!" You can negotiate with your inner-critic by asking it to allow you to prove yourself before it makes a judgment of whether or not you can do something.

Surrounding yourself with people that can encourage you and foster positivity will also change your inner-critic's opinion. Often times, hearing positive compliments from other people hold a heavier weight in the eyes of your inner-critic compared to you telling your inner-critic the same thing. Try spending time with people who are supportive of your goals and the changes that you are looking to make in your life. It will make your journey a little bit easier.

Step 7: Teach Your Inner-Critic to Be Supportive

The last and final step is training your inner-critic to become more supportive. We have now learned how to acknowledge our inner-critic, challenge the, and to negotiate with them. Now, we have to teach it to be supportive. So how do we do this? It sounds very airy-fairy, but it is through the process of repetition. Tell your inner-critic whenever you catch it in the act of telling you something negative, to tell you something positive instead. Don't just tell your inner-critic to "tell me something positive!", be very specific about what you are asking.

For instance, using our public speaking example, if your inner-critic is telling you that you are going to embarrass yourself and everyone will laugh at you, you can first prove it wrong by using evidence-based arguments, negotiate with it to let you try it out, and then ask for its support by saying "This is a difficult challenge for me, and I want to overcome it. I need you to be by my side, regardless of the outcome." Remember, your inner-critic is just another version of yourself. Be kind to it even if it's not kind to you. Showing yourself, kindness is very important in our case.

CONCLUSION

I first would like to ask you to give yourself a pat on the back for taking the initiative to read this book to get help and to finish it. As you may have learned by reading this book, it's not easy to gather motivation to get something done that benefits your long-term self and not your immediate-self. By picking up this book and learning brand new things to help you be more productive is a huge step in the right direction. Throughout this book, you learned the psychology of procrastination, why people procrastinate so often, cognitive behavioral therapy, how cognitive behavioral therapy can help overcome procrastination, the vicious cycle of procrastination, your inner-critic, and how to change your inner-critic. These are all intensive topics that should have given you a well-rounded understanding of why people procrastinate in the first place and the most effective methods to overcome it.

Consistency is really the key here when you are looking to improve something in your mind. We learned about how habits are the engrained neural pathways in our brain that become more ingrained over time. If it took you 10 years to get into the bad habit of eating junk food all the time, it'd likely take you many years to get out of it. Although that sounds daunting, I promise you it will get easier the more consistent you are with it. Learning good habits is just the same. By being consistent with your mindfulness and changing your unhelpful thinking styles, you will get into the habit of having a positive mindset over a bad one. Once your good habits are deeply engrained, you won't even have to think about it anymore. That's the level that you want to get to.

Not every technique works perfectly for everyone. Some people find cognitive behavioral therapy to be extremely effective, but some people may not find it as useful. If that's the case, try one of the other methods that you learned in this book. You can just try the simple, practical guide to overcoming procrastination that doesn't involve as much technical work as CBT does. Although that method is not as effective in terms of preventing procrastination, it is effective in helping you manage it and overcome it. If you find that one or two techniques are not working for you, try something else! Pick one that feels the most natural to you. Keep in mind, however, that these techniques require several weeks of practice in order to be effective, so just don't just switch techniques if you don't see any progress after the first few days.

One important thing that I want to note before ending this off is that everyone has lapses and relapses when it comes to changing their mind structure. Just like people who are battling with anxiety, depression, or self-esteem, people who are battling with procrastination may relapse into their bad habits sometimes. This is completely okay. The point here is that you forgive yourself, and you continue practicing the techniques that you have practiced this whole time. Just because you have relapsed once, twice, or ten times doesn't mean you have failed. There is no failure here. There is only forward movement. So if one day you decide to binge-watch your favorite Netflix series rather than working on a paper that's due in a week, that is okay. You may feel bad about it at the moment, but it does not mean you should give up on the process entirely. Simply accept the fact that you had a lapse, figure out what you did wrong at that moment, and apply it to your future growth.

So what's next after this book? Well, that's completely up to you! My advice to you will be to continue to practice the CBT techniques in this book even if you have mastered the art of not procrastinating. Using CBT to practice mindfulness and rewiring your own brain into one that fosters positivity will always bring good results to your life. Don't stop being mindful just because you haven't procrastinated in a while. Simply being mindful of your own thoughts and emotions produces a healthier lifestyle than someone who neglects thinking about their feelings and thought processes. Again, I'd like to thank you for taking the time to overcome procrastination with me. I hope you learned some valuable things that you can carry with you for the rest of your life. Feel free to spread the love and share some of the things you've learned in this book with your friends and family. Remember, it's important to let people know you are on a journey of overcoming procrastination so they can provide you the support and positivity you need to reach your goals.

APPENDIX

Worksheet #4.1 Sentence Completion

1. If I start to feel fear regarding starting a new task, I will acknowledge that I'm probably anticipating embarrassment (or any other negative emotions) about…

2. When considering whether my goals are "worth it", I will say…

3. When I let potential fear or embarrassment get in the way of completing tasks, I will ask myself these follow question to help minimize those emotions…

4. If I feel uncertain about doing a task, and I feel like I'm on the verge of making an excuse, I will resolve this by doing...

5. I know I have the ability to work towards my goals while also honoring my daily responsibilities by making these changes to my prioritization and time management...

6. Striving for these big goals that I have will help better me in different aspects of my life in these following ways...

Worksheet #5.1 Dysfunctional Thought Record

Date & Time When did this thought occur?	Situation What was the context? What other things were	Automatic Thought Describe your thought and rate how much you believed it between 0 - 100.	Emotion What feelings arose at this time? What was its intensity from 0-100?	Cognitive Distortion E.g. Catastrophizing, filtering, personalization....etc.	Alternative Thoughts What is a more realistic and positive thought?	Outcome Re-rate how much you believe the original thought and emotions from 0 -

Worksheet #5.2 Cognitive Restructuring

What I am thinking:	
Facts Supporting the Thought	Facts Contradicting the Thought
• • • • • • • • • • •	• • • • • • • • • •
Is thought based on evidence or opinion?	

Worksheet #6.1 Training Your Inner-Critic (Four-Step Guide)

Step 1: Revive Your Curiosity

1. What is my Inner-critic saying to me?

A:_____

2. What is my Inner-Critic saying about me specifically?

A:_____

3. When does my Inner-Critic say these things? Be as specific as possible.

A:_____

4. As a result of those things, what do I normally think about myself?

A:_____

5. What are the common patterns and themes that I recognize regarding my inner-critic?

A:_____

6. How do all these things together affect my overall behavior?

A:_____

7. What do all these thoughts say about me?
A:

8. Where do these opinions come from?
A:

9. Are these opinions factual, or are they all made up?
A:

10. Is it even appropriate to think this way in this certain situation?
A:_____

11. Where/when did I start learning to think this way?
A:_____

12. Are there any childhood experiences that stand out to me? Do I think that these experiences have an effect on the way I think now?
A:_____

_____
_____
_____
_____
_____
_____
_____
_____
_____

13. Is there anybody that may have instilled these thoughts into my mind?

A:_____
_____
_____
_____
_____
_____
_____
_____
_____
_____

14. Does this type of thinking even make sense, logically?

A:_____
_____
_____
_____
_____
_____
_____
_____
_____
_____

Step 2: Acknowledge Your Inner-critic

1. What is my inner-critic trying to protect me from?

A:_____

2. What does my inner-critic not want me to feel or experience?

A:_____

3. Why is this important to my inner-critic?

A:_____

4. Are the words my inner-critic is using critical or constructive?
A:_____

5. Are the words being used designed to help me improve or to criticize me?
A:_____

6. Are the words being used based on factual evidence? Or are they based on an opinion?
A:_____

7. If I take these words into consideration, where in my life might I need to make some changes?
A:_____

8. How else could I make changes in my life without all this resistance from my inner-critic?
A:_____

Step 3: Thank and Appreciate Your Inner-Critic

Dear Inner-Critic,

Thank you for always cautioning me of

_____
_____
_____
_____.

Thank you for always watching over me in

_____
_____
_____ situations.
I appreciate all the different times that you told me that I couldn't do

_____

_____, but I want to tell you that I am capable of doing_____

_____
_____.
Instead of telling me lies that you have heard from my childhood, or other people in my life, I want you to tell me constructive criticism such   as;

_____
_____
_____.

You are always welcome to give me feedback, but if you are acting stubborn, I will ignore you.

Sincerely,

_____

Step 4: Negotiate With Your Inner-Critic

Your Goal	What You Expect Your Inner-Critic to Say	How You Will Negotiate With Your Inner-Critic

RECOMMENDED READINGS

Barlow, D. H., Craske, M. G. (2000). Mastery of your anxiety and panic (3rd Edition). San Antonio, TX: The Psychological Corporation.

Barlow, D.H. (2002). Anxiety and Its Disorders: The Nature and Treatment of Anxiety and Panic (2nd Edition). London: Guilford Press

Bernard, M.E. (1991). Procrastinate Later! How To Motivate Yourself To Do It Now. Australia: Schwartz & Wilkinson.

Burka, J.B., & Yuen, L.M. (1983). Procrastination: Why You Do It, What To Do About It. US: DaCapo Press.

Burns, D.D. (1980). Feeling Good: The New Mood Therapy. New York: Signet

Clark D.A., Beck A.T. (2010). Cognitive Therapy of Anxiety Disorders The Guilford Press, New York London

Clark D.M. (1986). A cognitive approach to panic. Behav. Res. Ther. 24, No. 4. pp. 461-470.

Craske M. G., Barlow D. H. (2008). Panic Disorder and Agoraphobia. In Clinical Handbook of Psychological Disorders, Fourth Edition: A Step-by-Step Treatment Manual.

Craske, M.G., Barlow, D.H. (2001). Panic disorder and agoraphobia. In D.H. Barlow (Ed.), Clinical Handbook Of Psychological Disorders, Third Edition. New York: Guilford Press.

Ellis, A., & Knaus, W.J. (1977). Overcoming Procrastination. New York: Signet.

Ellis, A.E., and W.J. Knaus (1979). Overcoming Procrastination. New York: New American

Farmer R.E., Chapman A.L. (2008). Behavioral Interventions in Cognitive Behavior Therapy. Practical guidance for putting theory into action. American Psychological Association, Washington

Fentz H.N., Hoffart A., Jensen M.B., Arendt M., O'Toole M.S., Rosen-berg N.K., Hougaard E. (2013). Mechanisms of change in cognitive behaviour therapy for panic disorder: The role of panic self-efficacy and catastrophic misinterpretations. Behaviour Research and Therapy 5, 579 e 587.

Ferrari J. R., Johnson J. L., McCown W. G. (Eds.) (1995). Procrastination research, in Procrastination and Task Avoidance (Boston, MA: Springer;), 21–46.

Fiore, N. (1989). The Now Habit: A Strategic Program For Overcoming Procrastination And Enjoying Guilt-Free Play. New York: Penguin Group.

Flett A. L., Haghbin M., Pychyl T. A. (2016). Procrastination and depression from a cognitive perspective: an exploration of the associations among procrastinatory automatic thoughts, rumination, and mindfulness. J. Ration. Emot. Cogn. Behav. Ther. 34, 169–186. 10.1007/s10942-016-0235-1

Freedman S., Adessky R. (2009). Cognitive Behavior Therapy for Panic Disorder. Isr J Psychiatry Relat Sci, 46 No.4 251–256.

Harriot, J.L., and J.R. Ferrari (1996). Prevalence of Procrastination Among Samples of Adults. Psychological Reports 78:611-616.

Knaus, W. (2002). The Procrastination Workbook: Your Personalized Program For Breaking Free From The Patterns That Hold You Back. Oakland, CA: New Harbinger Publications Inc.

Knaus, W.J. (1979). Do It Now: How To Stop Procrastinating. New Jersey: Prentice-Hall Inc.
Library.

Nathan, P.R., Rees, C.S., Lim, L., & Smith, L.M. (2001). Mood Management – Anxiety: A Cognitive Behavioural Treatment Programme for Individual Therapy. Perth: Rioby Publishing.

Saulsman, L., & Nathan, P. (2008). Put Off Procrastinating. Perth, Western Australia: Centre for Clinical Interventions.

Teachman B.A., Marker C.D., and Clerkin E. M. (2010). Catastrophic misinterpretations as a predictor of symptom change during treatment for panic disorder. J. Consult, Clin. Psychol. December; 78(6): 964–973.

White, K.S. Barlow, D.H. (2002). Panic Disorder and Agoraphobia. In D.H. Barlow (Ed.), Anxiety and Its Disorders. Second Edition. New York: Guilford Press.

ABOUT THE AUTHOR

Antonio Matteo Bruscella is a licensed psychologist who specialized in cognitive-behavioral treatments for anxiety, depression, insomnia, and other conditions. Dr. Bruscella is Chairman and founding member of the Lucana Association of Psychology and Cognitive Behavioural Therapy (ALPTCC) and member of the British Psychological Society (BPS).

Printed in Great Britain
by Amazon